Absolute Surrender

by

Andrew Murray

Rickfords Hill Publishing Ltd.

Published by

RICKFORDS HILL PUBLISHING LTD.

24 High Street, Winslow, Buckingham, MK18 3HF, UK.

www.rhpbooks.co.uk

First Published 1895
RHP Edition 2015

ISBN: 978-1-905044-41-2

Printed and bound in Great Britain
by CPI Group (UK) Ltd, Croydon CR0 4YY

Contents

Preface

At the request of those who have arranged for the publication of these addresses, I write a few words by way of introduction. I gladly avail myself of the opportunity to point out to those readers who may not have attended such Conventions as those in which they were delivered, what the special object is for which they were first spoken and are now published.

I know not that I can do this better than by pointing to the origin of the Keswick Convention. Canon Battersby had for more than twenty years been an earnest evangelical minister, known and esteemed for his piety. But that piety bore in his heart the mark which so much of the religion of God's children has—the consciousness of not living well pleasing to God. The painful sense of continual failure and defeat in the battle with sin, the frequent loss of the light and joy of God's presence, made that perfect peace and abiding communion of which the Word speaks an impossibility. Before the great Oxford Convention of 1873, he had been deeply stirred by the tidings that there were those who could testify of victory over sin, and continuous walking in the light, as the rule of their Christian experience. He saw that there were promises in God's Word to warrant this, but he knew not how to inherit them. At the Convention he heard an address on Faith as a resting on Christ's Word, and saw that in that faith he might claim and receive the power of Christ to do in him what he had hitherto thought impossible. The Spirit of God, who gave him to see this, gave him also to accept it, and he was ready to testify at once of what God had done for him.

The Keswick Convention had its origins in the desire to give his testimony in wider circles. With others he spoke of the old life they too had once lived, of the new life and joy God had now bestowed, and of the simple way in which through faith they had found the passage from the one to the other. The blessing that followed was great. Numbers who had longed for a better life than they had led found the help they needed. In the power and joy of the Holy Spirit an atmosphere was created, of which the presence is felt to this day. The intensely personal tone in the call to confession and surrender of what was wrong in the past, the joyous testimony to the blessedness of what Christ actually had made possible, the simple and trustful appeal to come and by a single act of faith at once prove God's faithfulness and power, brought to many a message and a blessing they had never found in the ordinary preaching.

And why have I written this? Simply to point out and press home upon my readers the three great thoughts which mark the Conventions for the Deepening of the Spiritual Life, in which these addresses attempt to illustrate.

The first aim is always to discover the evil of the low spiritual state which so many look as the only possible Christian life. Nothing does more harm in the Church of Christ than the secret thought that obedience is impossible. Until believers see the error of this, and begin to look

upon the life of continual failure as something sinful
and unallowable, no preaching will profit much. The
first lesson must be, that a walk after the flesh, that a life
continually yielding to self-will, is contrary to what God
absolutely requires and actually bestows.

The second aim of this teaching is to make clear that
God has in very deed made a provision in Christ, the
Almighty Saviour from sin and in the Holy Spirit dwelling
in us to make Christ with His saving power every moment
real within us, by which the life of victory and rest and
fellowship can be maintained. It is only as we see in
God's Word this life prepared for us that we can have the
courage to hope for it.

Then comes the third point, that the transition from the
old life of stumbling and oft interrupted fellowship can be
by one step, and in one moment. And that only, but most
certainly, because it is nothing but a new act of faith in
Christ, trusting Him to work in us what we have failed to
do ourselves.

I cannot too earnestly request the reader of this book
to regard it all as a very simple personal appeal. Let him
ask God to deal with him, and show him whether he is
indeed walking in the path of absolute surrender and close
fellowship which is called. If any child of God reads the
book as a scholar, to know certain truths more clearly, or
as a Christian simply desirous of being edified, he will
very probably be disappointed. Let him read it as a sinner
wanting deliverance from sin, and he will very probably
be blessed.

With the humble prayer that God may by His Spirit
bless the written page, as it has pleased Him to bless the

spoken word when we were gathered in His presence, I
commit the book and its readers to His holy care.

ANDREW MURRAY
Wimbledon, 2nd December 1895

1

"Be Filled With the Spirit"

The words from which I wish to speak are well known:
you will find them in Acts 2:4, *"They were all filled
with the Holy Ghost"*; and in Ephesians 5:18, *"Be filled
with the Spirit."* The one text is a narrative; it tells us what
actually happened. The other text is a command; it tells us
what we ought to be.

In case there should be any doubt in our minds about it
being actually a command, "Be not drunk with wine, but
be filled with the Spirit."

Now, I am sure there is not one here who, if I asked
him, Do you try to obey that command, "Be not drunk
with wine"? would not answer at once, "Of course, as
a Christian, I obey that command." But now, as to the
other "Be filled with the Spirit," have you obeyed that
command? Is that the life you are living? If not, the
question comes at once, Why not?

And then comes another question, Are you willing to
take up that command tonight, and to say: By God's help
I am going to obey. I will not give myself any rest until
I have obeyed that command, until I am filled with the
Spirit.

I want at the very commencement to say that it is here a
simple question of listening to a command of God's Holy

Spirit, in His Word. We do not want to occupy or interest you with what we have got to say about this filling of the Holy Spirit, because that may lead you away into notions and conceptions which are really of no value towards the realization of the one special object we are now aiming at; but we want to begin at once by saying God has this message to every Christian in this place: My child, I want you to be filled with the Spirit. Let your answer be: Father, I want it too; I am ready; I yield myself to obey my God; let me be filled with Thy Spirit tonight.

And lest anyone should have a wrong impression as to what it is to be filled with the Spirit, just let me say that it does not mean a state of high excitement, or of absolute perfection, or a state in which there will be no growth. No. Being filled with the Spirit is simply this: having my whole nature yielded to His power. When the whole soul is yielded to the Holy Spirit, God Himself will fill it.

Now the question I want to ask is, *What is needed in order to be filled with the Spirit?* The question is of the utmost importance, and if we try to find the answers that have to be given, it may help to search us. We prayed, in the hymn we have just sung, that God might *search* us, and those answers will help each of us to look into our heart and life, and say: Am I in that condition in which God can fill me with the Spirit? I think the answers we shall find may also help to encourage us. There may be souls here who may say honestly, as we go on step by step: Thank God, I am ready for that; and they may perhaps see that they are kept back from this full blessing just by some ignorance, or prejudice, or unbelief, or wrong thoughts of what the blessing is.

Now, I do not see how we can better find the answer to our question than by looking at the way in which Christ prepared the disciples for the Day of Pentecost. You know what is done in heathen countries where the missionary preaches. Converts come to him, and he forms a baptismal class, and there are cases in which he keeps these young converts for a year, or longer at times, in the baptismal class, to educate and train and test them, and to prepare them for the Christian life. And, brethren, Jesus had His disciples three years in His baptismal class, and they had to go through a time of training and preparation. It was not a magic thing, an arbitrary thing, the Holy Spirit coming down upon them. They were prepared for it. John the Baptist told them what was to come. He not only preached the Lamb of God who was to shed His blood, but he preached and he tells us that it was by special revelation from God that He on whom he saw the Holy Spirit descend would baptize with the Holy Ghost.

And now, wherein consisted the training of those disciples? Wherein consisted their preparation for the baptism of the Holy Spirit? I ask you, first, to remember that *they were men who had forsaken all to follow Jesus.*

You know the Lord Jesus went to one and said, Forsake your net; and to another, Leave that place in the receipt of custom, and come and follow Me. And they did it, and they could afterwards say by the mouth of Peter, "Lord we have forsaken all and followed thee": their homes, their families, their good name. Men mocked and laughed at them, men called them *the disciples of Jesus*, and when He was despised and hated they were hated too. They identified themselves with Him, they gave themselves up entirely to do His bidding.

1. There is the first step in the way to the baptism of the Holy Spirit. We must forsake all to follow Christ.

I am not now speaking about forsaking *sin*; that you have to do when you are converted. But there is something that has a far wider meaning. Many Christians think that they receive Jesus as someone who can save them and help them, but virtually they deny Him as Master. They think they have a right to have their own will in a thousand things. They speak very much what they like, they do very much what they like, they use their property and possessions as they like; they are their own masters, and they have never dreamed of saying: Jesus, I just forsake all to follow Thee.

And yet this is the demand of Christ. Christ hath such infinite riches and glory that He deserves it, and Christ is such a heavenly, spiritual, divine gift that unless we give up everything, our hearts cannot be filled with Him. And so Jesus comes and says: Forsake all and follow Me.

I was at Johannesburg last year at the Convention. Hear just one simple story of what has been done there in God's kingdom. I had some services, and on an afternoon when there was a gathering of believers to testify of what God had done for them, one poor woman rose and told how, some six months before, she had received such a wonderful blessing through the inflowing of God's Spirit. At a consecration meeting which she had attended in a very poor neighbourhood, the minister who was giving an address asked who were ready to give themselves up entirely for Jesus. He used the words, "Suppose He wanted you to go to China, or to give up your wife and children, would you be willing to do it?" And she said earnestly, "I *did* want to say, I will give up everything to Jesus, but I could not. When he asked those to rise who were willing, I was in a great state, but still I could not remain sitting, and I rose and said: Yes, I will give up everything. Yet I felt as if I could not give up my husband and children. I went home, but I could not sleep; I could not rest, for there was the struggle; must I give up *everything*? Yet I *wanted* to do it for the sake of Jesus. It was past midnight, and I said: Lord, yes, for Thee *everything!* And the joy and the power of the Spirit flowed into my heart." She testified, and her minister testified of her too, that she walked in the joy of the Lord.

Dear friends, you have, perhaps, never said it, because you never thought it was needed; but say it tonight. Are you willing to say, "O Christ, let me be filled with the Holy Spirit; I will give up anything and everything; accept of my surrender"?

Each of us must examine himself. Some have never thought it a necessity to do it. Some have never understood what it meant when Jesus said that except a man hate father and mother, and wife and children, and houses and lands, and forsake them for His sake and the gospel's, he is not worthy of Him. Is not this the reason of your feeble life, the reason that the Holy Spirit does not fill your being? you have never forsaken all to follow Christ.

2. A second thought. They were not only men who had forsaken all to follow Jesus, but they were *intensely attached to Him*. Jesus had said, "If ye love Me, keep My commandments, and I will pray the Father, and He will send the Comforter." And they *did* love Him intensely.

They had seen Him crucified, but their hearts could not be separated from Him. They had no hope or joy or comfort on earth without Him; and, oh, friends, it is this that is so often wanting in our religion. We trust Jesus and His work on Calvary; we trust Him as our only Saviour; that is well, and may be sufficient to bring salvation. But the thought that religion means that Jesus, the unseen One, shall be my Friend and Guide and Keeper all the day, my Leader and Master whom I obey alas! how much religion is there in which such a thought is never found!

If you ask what the "Keswick teaching" is, that, I think, is one of its strong elements. Some two or three years ago a young lady missionary came out to South Africa, and she spoke so much of the blessing she had received at Keswick. She told me how, from a child, she had loved the Lord Jesus, and been educated in a circle of godly friends, and a godly home, but what a difference it had made to her when she found what it is to receive the deeper blessing. I said to her, "You have now from your childhood lived in a bright, godly atmosphere; do tell me what you think is the difference between the life you then lived and the life you entered upon afterwards." Her answer was simple and ready and bright; "It is just this", she said, *"the personal fellowship with Jesus."* Oh, friends, there must be a beginning of that. Some people would forsake everything for the sake of their religion. For a false religion multitudes have given up all. Some people would forsake all for the sake of their church. Some people would forsake all for the sake of their fellow men. But that is not what is wanted. We want to forsake all for the sake of Jesus, to let Him come into our life and take possession of our heart. Is your life one of tender personal attachment to Jesus, and of joy in Him? I do not ask whether your attainment in this matter be perfect, but I do ask, can you say honestly: It is what I am striving after, it is what I have given myself up to, it is what I long for above everything. Jesus Christ must have me every day and all the day?

3. A third thought: these disciples were *men who had been led to despair of themselves.* At the beginning of their three years' class of instruction they had to give up all they possessed; but it was only at the end of that time that they began to give up themselves. They had given up their nets, and their homes, and their friends, and that was right; but all the three years how strong self was! How often Jesus spoke to them about humility! But they could not understand Him. Time after time there was contention amongst them as to who should be chief. At the Supper table they were still talking about that who will be first amongst us? They had not given up self. As was made manifest more than once, how little they lived in the Spirit of Jesus!

But Christ taught them and trained them. He revealed to them, time after time, what the sin of pride is, and what the glory of humility is, and when He died upon the Cross, they died a terrible death too. Think of Peter, the impetuous disciple, having denied his Lord. Do not you think that in all the sorrows of those three days, from the crucifixion day to the resurrection day, the deepest and the bitterest was this shame at the thought of how he had treated his Lord? Then he learned to despair of himself. At the Supper table how self-confident he had been!

"Although all shall be offended, yet will not I." But Jesus took him down with Him into death and the grave, and then Peter felt that there was in him, indeed, no good thing. He had learned to despair of himself.

Some of you may say: I think I have given up all for Jesus; my property, my home, my friends, my position, and I think I do love Him, but somehow it won't come right. I do not get the blessing I need. Dear friends, are you willing that God, with His searchlight, should discover to you how much there is in you of self will and self trust. Take, for instance, your judgment of people; how you speak just what you like, and what you think right, and have not yet learned to study the humility and tenderness and gentleness of Jesus. That is *self*. You work for Him. You try to do good, but all the time it is really your own working. You as a Christian are doing the work, and you look to God to help and bless. But that cannot be. God must first bring each one of us down into the place of death.

Do you know what the death of Jesus means? It means this—that Jesus said to His Father, in effect: Here is My life, so precious to Me, My life which has been sinless. I have yielded it to Thee in death. He went into the grave saying, "Into Thy hands I commit," I give away, I entrust, "My Spirit." And you know what happened. Because He gave up His life so entirely, and sank into the thick darkness of death and the grave, God raised Him up into a new life and a new glory and a new power. God raised Him from the grave to glory. It was the death that was the secret of the resurrection. And, believer, understand that if you want to be filled with the Spirit and the risen life of glory, you must first die to self. The apostles were men who had been brought to an utter self-despair, men who had lost all, and who were ready to receive all from God in heaven.

4. One thought more: these apostles were *men who had accepted the promise of the Spirit from Jesus in faith*. You know that on that last night Christ had spoken to them about the Holy Spirit more than once, and that when He was ready to ascend, He said again, "Ye shall be baptized with the Holy Ghost not many days hence." If you had asked those disciples, What does that mean? I am sure they could not have told you. They did not understand it, perhaps, so much as we do. They had no conception of what would come. But they took the word of Jesus, and if they had any need for talking or arguing during those ten days, I am sure they said: If while He was on earth He did such wonderful things for us, now that He is in glory He will do things infinitely more wonderful. And they waited for that.

Now, I want you to accept this promise by faith, and to say: That promise of the filling of the Holy Ghost is for *me*. I accepted it at the hand of Jesus. You may not understand it; you may not feel as you would like to feel; you may feel yourself weak and sinful and far away from Jesus; but you may come tonight and say and you have a right to say it, That promise is for *me*. Are you ready to do so? Are you ready in faith to trust the promise, and the word, and the love of Jesus? I am sure there are believers here who are struggling to find out what their want is, who possibly have given themselves in the dust. But the want is, that they have not learned simply to say: He has promised, and He will do it.

Let me say, for your encouragement tonight, that when

you get a promise from God it is worth just as much as a fulfilment. A promise brings you into direct contact with God. Only honour Him by trusting the promise and obeying Him, and if there is any preparation that you still need, God knows about it; and if there is anything that is to be opened up to you He will do it, if you count upon Him to do it. Trust the promise, and say: This fullness of the Holy Spirit is for me.

5. And then, the last step with the disciples was this; *On the strength of that promise they waited in united prayer*. And that is what we are here for in union with each other to wait on God in prayer. They waited, they prayed with one accord; prayer and supplication went up to God mingled with praise. They expected—and take you away this lesson—they expected God in heaven to do something. I wish I could tell you the importance of that! I find Christians and I have found it in my own experience who read, and understand, and think, and wish, and want to claim, and want to take, and want to get, and yet what they crave for eludes their grasp. And why? Because they do not wait for God to give it.

Do not look to what we say, or to what you think and understand, with a view of getting a blessing out of that. *Look to God, and expect God to do something*. It is not enough to believe. I find many people mistake faith for the blessing that faith is intended to bring. By faith I am to "inherit the promises." Oh, believe and trust God; then look to Him to give the blessing. Be ye "filled with the Holy Ghost."

2

The Blessedness of Being Filled With the Holy Spirit

I wish to try and put before you what the blessedness is of a life filled with the Holy Spirit. I spoke two nights ago about the way in which the disciples were led to receive the blessing; but let us tonight look at the blessedness of being filled with the Spirit. It may please God to make our desire so strong, and to make us see so clearly, *This is just what I need, I cannot live longer without it*, that He may bring us to receive, this very night, more than we ever expected. He is a God who is willing and able to do above what we can ask or think. I do not think I can put the blessedness of being filled with the Spirit more clearly before you than by just pointing to the wonderful change which Pentecost made in the lives of the disciples. I think that is one of the most wonderful object-lessons in the whole of Scripture—those twelve men under Christ's training for three years, and yet remaining, apparently, at such a distance from the life they ought to live; and then all at once, by the blessed incoming of the Holy Spirit, being made just what God wanted them to be.

Look first at *the change that Pentecost wrought in their relationship to Jesus*. During His life on earth with them they could not have Him within them. There He was outside, separated from them, very near, very loving; and yet, if I may say so with deep reverence, what a failure Christ's teaching of them was until the Holy Spirit came! Christ taught them humility, time after time. He said, "Learn of Me, for I am meek and lowly in heart." He said, time after time, "He that humbled himself shall be exalted." Yet at the Holy Communion table there they were, still contending which of them should be chief. Christ did not conquer their pride. This was not for the want of divine teaching. Why was it, then? It was because of one thing: Christ was still outside of them, and He could not get into their heart to dwell there. It was impossible; the time had not come, and there they had the divine, almighty, blessed Redeemer along with them, but still outside. And how different they were from Him! To teach us that no outward instruction, even from Christ Himself, or His words in Holy Scripture, can bring us the true and full blessing, till the Holy Spirit works it in us. But what a change took place on the day of Pentecost! "At that day ye shall know that I am in you." What does that mean? Christ in us, just the same as we are in this tent? No, we are in the tent, but we can go out of it again, and we do not suffer anything by it. I live in a house, but I can leave that house and go elsewhere. The tent and the house and I are not vitally, organically connected. But the Lord Jesus came to be—I say it with reverence,—part of those disciples, to fill their heart and thought and affection; and what Peter and James and John had, when they had Christ alongside of them, you and I have in a much larger measure, if we have the living Christ within us.

And how did that change come? By the Holy Spirit. "At that day" when the Spirit come "ye shall know that I am in you"; for the Father will love you, and I will love you, and we will come and make our abode in you. Oh! Does not your heart long for it? I have thought and thought of Jesus in Bethlehem, and of Jesus on Calvary, and of Jesus upon the throne, and I have worshiped and loved and rejoiced exceedingly in Him; but all the time I wanted something better and something deeper and something nearer. Is not what you want this: to have the loving Jesus within yourselves? And that is what the Holy Spirit will give you, and that is why we want to plead with you tonight. Will you not give up yourselves for this blessing to be filled with the Spirit, that the blessed Jesus may be able to take possession of you? Is not that what your heart longs for? Jesus *within*; the very Jesus, who is the Almighty One, who died on the Cross and sits upon the throne, condescending to be our life?

And that is what the Spirit comes for. Jesus said, "He will glorify Me, for He will take of Mine and show it unto you." And what is the glory of Jesus? His love and His power. And the Holy Spirit will reveal Christ in us, so that the wonderful love of Christ shall be a possession and a reality in its divine nearness, and that power of Christ shall have the mastery within us. You know that wonderful prayer in Ephesians 3, that the Father might strengthen them with might by the Spirit in the inner man, that Christ might dwell in their heart. The mighty power of the Holy Spirit can do it. The Holy Spirit makes Jesus present with us.

And then, the second thought in connection with the

change wrought in the disciples: not only was Jesus outside
of them, but Jesus was not always with them. They could
not every moment be with Him. You remember how, at
one time, He sent them across the sea, and He stayed on
the mountain to pray. You remember how, at another time,
He took three of them with Him up into the mountain, and
the others stayed down below; and there they had to meet
the Pharisees, and they could not cast out the evil spirit.
There came times of separation, and at last there came
that terrible death, that awful separation from them in this
world. Yes, Christ was their life: sometimes with Christ,
and sometimes not with Him; sometimes near Him, and
sometimes the crowd pressing around Him, and they could
not get to Him. But, ah! friends, *the presence of Jesus by
the Holy Ghost is meant to be unbroken, continual, and
forever*. Is not that what your heart longs for? Do not you
know what it is sometimes to live a week or a month in a
joy that makes your heart sing all the day? And the change
comes, and the cloud and the darkness come and you do
not know why it is: sometimes with bodily sickness or
depression, sometimes with the cares and the difficulties
of this life, sometimes with the consciousness of your
own failure. Oh, child of God, would that I could tell it
you and see it myself aright! Jesus does love you; He
does not wish to be separated from you one minute; He
cannot bear it. We want to believe in that love of Jesus. No
mother ever so delighted in the baby she has in her arms
as does the Christ of God in you. He wants to be most
intimate with you, and to have most unceasing fellowship
with you. Take that in, beloved believer, and say tonight:
If that be possible, God helping me, I must have Jesus

always dwelling in my heart.

Another thought. *Look at the change it made in their own inner life.* It was, up to Pentecost, a life of failure and of weakness. I have spoken of their pride. Christ had to reprove them for their pride, time after time. You know how they longed to be faithful to Him, and yet their pride and their self confidence was the cause of continual failure. Peter said to Him, "Lord, I will never deny Thee," and all the others said the same; and yet within a few hours they did it, just as the result of pride and self-confidence. They did not know the evil of their own nature. Jesus had done everything to teach them humility, but He had failed, and hence their weakness. Peter had said "I will go with Thee to prison and to death," but at the word of a maid-servant he began to swear and to declare that he never knew the Man. What utter weakness! But what a change when Pentecost came! I will not say they had victory over sin, for I do not think it came in the way of direct fighting. But when the Holy Spirit the Spirit of God became their life, they were filled with the might and the power of the living Jesus, the Saviour from sin.

You know, dear friends, that the great work of Jesus is to take away sin. And how does He take it away? Many Christians just look upon Him as taking it away on the Cross. Others get a step beyond that, and say: He takes it away from heaven; He cleanses and keeps me. But the true taking away of sin is this: if the light comes in, the darkness is expelled. It is the presence of Jesus, indwelling by the Holy Spirit, that can make us holy. And the disciples, what a change came over them! See now how boldly, time after time, they can speak in the presence of those who threaten them with death. "We must obey God rather than men," they said. They go to prison, and there they can sing praises to God at midnight. Oh the wonderful change in their life that the Holy Spirit wrought!

And what does that teach us? We very often speak about the self-life, and the life of the Holy Spirit. Have you said to God—perhaps you have said it often—"Lord, how can I be rid of this self-life?" Well, has it been *discovered* to you? Has God's finger reached the deep place of your heart, and have you been brought to say: O God, my failure is all my self-confidence, self-will, self-pleasing? There is that accursed self that will have its say in everything, and there is no power that can expel that but the power of the presence of Jesus.

You may get troubled about some theological definition, as to how it is all done, as to how much sin there remains, and how much there is cast out, but what we want you to believe is this: that though you cannot explain and expound all, believe that the Spirit of holiness which will be given is the holiness of Jesus in your heart, and be content with that. Filled with the Spirit, you have within you the power of the holiness of God to do the blessed work of sanctification.

And then, the third thought in regard to this wonderful blessedness of being filled with the Spirit. Look at *the love that united them into one body*. I spoke a little while ago about their contention. There was selfishness among them, often want of love; but when the Holy Spirit came down do not look only at what He did for each one of them individually. He moulded them into one body, and they felt conscious that they were the members of one

Lord Jesus, and they loved each other, so that they did things which were utterly unheard of at that time. Though perfect strangers of each other, most of them, they began to sell their goods and give away their property, and to say they had all things in common. This was the result of the Holy Spirit having come down, as the very love of God in heaven, to dwell in their hearts.

And do not you find that your greatest difficulty in life is your relation to your fellow-Christians? Is not that our first temptation to sin—our intercourse with our fellow Christians? Very often, people who have to work together differ in temperament and character, and how easily friction comes in! There are people who differ in regard to some theological truth or practical way of doing Christ's work, and how they speak or write against each other! Alas, what separations there are in Christ's Church on earth! Even amongst those who are professing to love God, and professing holiness and entire consecration, what divisions unceasingly come! It is such a sad thing. How many earnest Christians there are who have so much to say one about another! They can point out where I am wrong, and I can point out where they are wrong; but how few there are of Christians, differing from each other distinctly, who can say, "Above all our differences there is a unity which we must express; we want continual fellowship in the presence of our one Father."

Do you want to have a heart overflowing with love to every child of God, to all the children of God outside your own circle? Do you want a heart of love that can set others on fire? Do you want the very love of heaven to flow out from you? Do you want the self-sacrificing love of

Jesus to take possession of you, so that you can bear and forbear, so that with the long suffering and tenderness and gentleness, and the very meekness of Christ, the Lamb of God, you are willing to be the helper and servant of everyone, however unlovable or unlovely? Then you need to be filled with the Spirit. Cry for that, claim that, accept that, rest not till you have it. The Spirit is the Spirit of God's love, and is the Spirit of the crucified love of Jesus. If we receive the Holy Ghost, the love of God will be shed abroad in our hearts, and God will melt us into one as never before.

And then, just one more thought, and it is *in regard to their work*. See what a difference Pentecost made! And I suppose we all feel, at least many of us feel, that is one of the important things in connection with speaking about being filled with the Holy Spirit. I doubt not but there are many workers here who can thank God for the way He has led them on, but who still feel that they want something very different. Joy in speaking of Jesus, they say, I have not got that always, the consciousness that God is using me as one of His instruments. Yet that is what God wants every worker to have.

Do not you feel that it would be an unutterable joy always to work in that spirit of absolute humility and dependence and nothingness, and with it all, a childlike trust that God will use you? Oh, how am I to get that? Look at the apostles, look at the disciples. I read that the Lord Jesus sent them out to do three things—to preach the gospel, to heal the sick, and to cast out devils; when they came back, they told about the two last—the healing of the sick and the casting out of devils; but I do not hear them tell about conversions. I do not think their preaching of the gospel really helped very much. It had to be done, but I do not know that it produced much result.

But when the Day of Pentecost came, listen to their preaching of the gospel—not only to Peter's; they were all proclaiming the mighty works of God. What a blessing came! And it went on and on. What boldness they had, and what largeness of heart!

How they went on to Samaria and to Caesarea, and then to Antioch, and there waited upon God; and how within a very few years the gospel had been brought into Europe! It was the power of the Holy Spirit that did it. And we want that power for our work, and spiritual light and wisdom to see the large fields of work that are before us, even in our immediate neighbourhood.

I thank God for all the interest He is awakening in heathendom and foreign missions, but I am afraid there is something that is getting neglected. And what is that? I thank God for all the interest there is in Darkest England, in the poor neglected ones, in the drunkards and those who are in danger of becoming drunkards, and in the poor outcast. But your middle classes, your richer and higher classes—is there power in your Christianity to take the gospel to them boldly? Are not many of you members of churches and congregations, where you sit Sunday by Sunday with multitudes around you, of whom you know that they are unconverted? Is there not a need of divine wisdom and power to fit us for this work? Do we not need divine light and inspiration? Do we not need power, with a new love and boldness to pray and wait and work, and to see that not only those who are in China, or in Africa, or in other parts of the world shall have the gospel, but that the gospel shall be brought to those with whom we are associated every day? We thank God that during the last thirty years He has aroused Christians to work as never before; but let us understand that it is but a beginning, and if Christians will hold counsel with God, and wait upon God in prayer, and say to God that they are ready for His work, is not God able to do far more than He has wrought hitherto?

But one thing is needed. The Spirit did it all, on the day of Pentecost and afterwards. It was the Spirit who gave the boldness, the Spirit gave the wisdom, the Spirit gave the message, and the Spirit gave the converting power.

And now, I speak to all workers, especially to those who feel the need of power to work, and I say, My brother, my sister, is not your whole heart ready to say, That is what I want. I see it. Jesus did not send me to the warfare on my own charges; He did not bid me go and preach and teach in my own strength; Jesus meant me to have the fullness of the Holy Ghost. Whether I have a little Sunday school class or a Bible class, or some larger work, the one thing I need is the power of the Holy Ghost, to be filled with the Spirit.

Let me conclude by asking, Are we all prepared now to receive this from our Jesus? He loves to give it. God delights in nothing so much as to honour His Son, and it is honour to Jesus when souls are filled with the Holy Ghost, because then He proves what He can do for them. Shall we not claim it?

Just let me give you four very little words as steps. Let now everyone who longs for this blessing say, first of all,

I must be filled. Say it to God in the depth of your heart. God commands it; I cannot live my life as I should live without it.

Then, say as the second step: *I may be filled.* It is possible the promise is for me. Settle that, and let all doubt vanish. These apostles, once so full of pride and of self-life, were filled with the Holy Spirit because they clave unto Jesus. And with all your sinfulness, if you will but cling to Him you *may be filled.*

Then thirdly, say: *I would be filled.* To get the "pearl of great price" you must sell all, you must give up everything. You are willing, are you not? Everything, Lord, if I may only have that. Lord, I would have it from Thee tonight.

And then comes the last step: *I shall be filled.* God longs to give it; I shall have it. Never mind whether it do not come tonight, because God is preparing you for it tomorrow. But say, *I shall be filled.* If I entrust myself to Jesus He cannot disappoint me. It is His very nature, it is His work in heaven, it is His delight to give souls the Holy Spirit in full measure. Oh, claim it tonight; *I shall.* My God, it is so solemn, it is almost awful; it is too blessed and too true Lord, wilt Thou not do it? My trembling heart says, *I shall be filled* with the Holy Spirit. Oh, say to God, "*Father, I shall*, for the name of my Saviour is Jesus, who saves from all sin, and who fills with the Holy Spirit. Glory to His name!"

3

Carnal and Spiritual

You will find the words from which I want to speak to you in 1 Corinthians 3:1–4 *"And I, brethren, could not speak unto you as unto spiritual, but as unto carnal, even as unto babes in Christ."*

The Apostle commences the chapter by telling these Corinthians that there are two stages of Christian experience. Some Christians are *carnal*, some are *spiritual.* By the discernment which God's Spirit gave the Apostle, he saw that the Corinthians were carnal, and he wanted to tell them so. You will find the word *carnal* four times in these four verses.

The Apostle felt that all his preaching would do no good if he talked about spiritual things to men who were unspiritual. They were Christians, real Christians, babes in Christ; but there was one deadly fault—they were carnal. So the Apostle seems to say: I cannot teach you spiritual truth about the spiritual life, you cannot take it in. But that was not because they were stupid. They were very clever, and full of knowledge, but unable to understand spiritual teaching. That teaches us this simple lesson that all the trouble in the Church of Christ among Christians who sometimes get a blessing and lose it again, is just because they are *carnal*, and all that we need if we want to keep the blessing is, that we become *spiritual*. We must choose what style of Christian life we would like to live, the *carnal* life or the *spiritual*. Choose the *spiritual*, and God will be delighted to give it you.

Now, if we are to understand this teaching we must begin by trying thoroughly to know what this carnal state is. I think I shall be able to point you to four very marked characteristics of the carnal state.

The *first* thing I have to say about it is, that *the carnal state is a state of protracted infancy*. It is a long time ago since you were converted, and you ought to have been a young man by this time, but you are still a babe in Christ. "I have fed you with milk, and not with meat; for hitherto ye were not able to bear it." You know what a babe is, and what a beautiful thing babyhood is. You cannot have a more attractive little thing than a child six months old, with its ruddy cheeks, its laughing and smiling face, the kicking of its little feet, and the movement of its little fingers. What a beautiful object! But suppose I saw such a child, and came back after six months and the child was not a bit bigger, the parents would begin to say, "We are afraid there is something the matter; the child won't grow." And if after three years I came back and saw there the baby no bigger yet, I should find the parents sad. They would tell me, "The doctor says there is some terrible disease about the child; it cannot grow. He says it is a wonder it is alive, and yet it does live." I come back after ten years, and there is that helpless infant, and still there is no growth.

You see, babyhood at the proper time is the most beautiful thing in the world, but babyhood continued too long is a burden and a sorrow, a sign of disease. And that was the state of many of those Corinthian Christians. They continued babes.

Now, what are the marks of a babe? There are specially two marks—a babe cannot help itself, and a babe cannot help others.

1. *A babe cannot help itself*, and that is the life of many Christians. They make their ministers spiritual nurses of babes. It is a solemn thing that those spiritual babes keep their ministers occupied all the time in nursing them and feeding them, and they never help themselves. They do not know themselves how to feed on Christ's Word, and the minister must feed them. They do not know what contact with God is, and the minister must pray for them. They do not know what it is to live as those who have God to help them; they always want to be nursed. Do take care that it does not become the reason why *you* come to the Convention to get your nurses to give you spiritual meat. God be praised for the preaching of the gospel and for the fellowship of the Convention. But, oh, you know what baby does—baby always keeps the house going, and very often mother cannot go out because there is baby, or the servant must be there to keep baby, or the nurse must be there; baby always occupies somebody. You cannot leave him alone. So there are many spiritual infants to whom ministers are always going, and who are always wanting some help. Instead of allowing themselves to be trained up to know their God and be strong, alas!

It is a protracted infancy. They cannot help themselves and can therefore not help others. Is not that just what we read in the Epistle to the Hebrews? There was the very same condition; we read that those who had been so long converted, and who ought to have been teachers, needed themselves to be taught the very rudiments of Christianity. And there are, as I have said, people who are always wanting to be helped instead of being a help to others.

For a little child, a spiritual babe of three month old, to be carnal and not to know altogether what sin is, and not yet to have got victory, it is, as Paul said, a thing not to be wondered at. But when a man continues, year after year, in the same state of always being conquered by sin, there is something radically wrong.

Nothing can keep a child in protracted infancy but disease of some sort. And if we have to say continually, "I am not spiritual," then do let us say, "O God, I am carnal; I am in diseased state, and want to be helped out of it."

2. The *second* mark of a carnal state is, that *sin and failure prove master*. Sin has the upper hand. What proof does Paul give that those people were carnal? He first charges them, and then he asks a question, "Among you there are envyings, and strifes, and divisions; are ye not carnal?" And then again, one says, "I am of Paul," and another, "I am of Apollos," and another, "I am of Cephas." Are you not carnal? asks Paul in effect; is not that evident? You just act like other men; you are not acting like heavenly, renewed men, who live in the power and love of the Holy Ghost. You know that God who loved us dwelled in light, and that love is the great commandment, and that the Cross of Christ is nothing but the evidence of God's love, and that the first fruit of the Holy Spirit is love. The whole of John's Gospel means *love*. And when men give away to their tempers and pride and envying and divisions; when you hear people saying sharp things about others; when

a man cannot open out his whole heart to a brother who has done him wrong, and forgive him; when a woman can speak about her neighbour with contempt as "That wretched thing," or say to another, "Oh, how I dislike that woman"—all these are fruits of the carnal spirit. Every touch of unlovingness is nothing but the *flesh*. The word carnal is a form of the Latin word for *flesh*, and all unlovingness is nothing but the fruit or work of the flesh.

The flesh is selfish and proud and unloving; therefore every sin against love is nothing but a proof that the man is carnal.

You say, "I have tried to conquer it, but I cannot." That is what I want to impress upon you. Do not try, while you are in the carnal state, to bear spiritual fruit. You must have the Holy Spirit in order to love, then the carnal will be conquered. He will give you the spirit to walk in love.

And it is not only true of the sins against love, but there are so many other sins. Take worldliness, which somebody says has "honeycombed the Church"; take the love of money; take the pursuit of business, making people sacrifice everything to the increase of riches; take so much of our life, the seeking after luxury and pleasure and position. What is all that but the flesh? It gratifies the flesh, it is exactly what the world thinks desirable and delights in, and if you live like the world it is a proof that the spirit of the world which is in the flesh is in you. The carnal state is proved by the power of sin.

Someone asked me recently, "How about the want of love of prayer?" He wanted to know how the art of loving fellowship with God could be attained. I said, "My brother, that cannot be attained in any way until you discover that it must come outside of the carnal state. The flesh cannot delight in God; that is your difficulty.

You must not say or write down a resolution in your journal that "I will pray more." *You* cannot force it. But let the axe come to the root of the tree; cut down the carnal mind. How can you cut it down? You cannot, but let the Holy Spirit of God come with the condemnation of sin and the Cross of Christ, and give over the flesh to the death, and the Spirit of God will come in. And then you will learn to love prayer and love God and love your neighbour, and you will be possessed of humility and spiritual-mindedness and heavenly mindedness. The carnal state is the root of every sin.

3. I come to the next point. If we want to know this carnal state, thoroughly, we must take very special notice that *the carnal state can coexist with great spiritual gifts*.

Remember, there is a great difference between spiritual gifts and spiritual graces and that is what many people do not understand. Among the Corinthians, for instance, there were very wonderful spiritual gifts. In the first chapter, Paul says, "I thank my God... that ye are enriched in all utterance and in all knowledge." That was something wonderful to praise God for. And in the Second Epistle he says in effect, "You do not come behind in any gift; see that you have the gift of liberality also." And in the twelfth chapter, how he speaks about the gifts of prophecy, and of faith that could remove mountains, and of knowledge as things that they were ardently seeking for; but he tells them these will not profit them without they have *love*. They delighted in the gifts, and did not care for the graces. But Paul shows them a more excellent way to learn to love and to be humble. Love is the greatest thing of all, for love is God-like above everything.

It is a very solemn thing for us to remember that a man may be gifted with prophecy, that a man may be a faithful and successful worker in some particular sphere among the poor and needy, and yet by the sharpness of his judgment and the pride that comes into them, and by other things, he may give proof that while his spiritual gifts are wonderful, spiritual graces are too often absent. Oh, take care that Satan does not deceive one of us with the thought, "But I work for God, and God blesses me, and others look up to me, and I am the means of helping others." Beloved fellow Christians, that a carnal man may have spiritual gifts is unspeakably solemn, because it must bring the most earnest and successful man to his knees before God with the thought, "Am I not, after all that God's Spirit works in me as a matter of gift, possibly giving way to the flesh, in lack of humility, or love, or purity, or holiness?" God search us and try us, for His name's sake.

4. A further point is this, *that the carnal state renders it impossible for a man to receive spiritual truth*. You see, perhaps, hundreds of Christians hungering for the Word, and they listen and they say, "What beautiful truths, what clear doctrines, what beautiful expositions of God's Word!" and yet they do not get helped one step; or they get helped for two or three weeks, and the blessing passes away. What is the reason? There is an evil at the bottom; the carnal state is hindering the reception of spiritual truth.

I am afraid that in our churches we often make a terrible mistake. We preach to carnal Christians what is only fit for spiritual men, and they think it so beautiful, and they take it into their heads and delight in it and say, "That is grand; what a view of the truth that man can give!" Yet their lives remain unchanged; they are carnal, with all the spiritual teaching they get. If there is one thing that we ought each to ask God at this Convention, it is this: "Lord deliver me from taking up spiritual teaching into a carnal mind!" The only evidence that you get a blessing is, that you are lifted out of the carnal into the spiritual state. God is willing to do it, and let us plead for it, and accept it.

So much for the meaning of carnal.

Now comes the very important and solemn question, *Is it possible for a man to get out of the carnal into the spiritual state? And how is it possible?* I want to answer that, and to point out the steps which must be taken to that end. I have asked God that He may help me to speak as simply as to little children, for I want to say to every honest, earnest heart that is longing to be spiritual, you can get out of the carnal state tonight into the spiritual state. And what is needed for that?

1. I think the first thing needed is, that *a man must have some sight of the spiritual life and some faith in it.* At bottom our hearts are so full of unbelief, without our knowing it, that we do not accept, as a settled matter, that we can become spiritual men tonight. We do not believe it.

I heard a most interesting story just before I left the Cape. I was talking to a man of much Christian experience about my coming over to England, and I said to him, "Tell me what is the state of the Christians in England. You have worked among them, and know them well." He replied, "I believe there is nothing so terrible amongst them as *unbelief*." Then he told me a story of a young man of high promise, who was in England working for Christ. That young man had great gifts, but my friend could not understand why, with all those gifts, he did not get more blessing. Well, these two men spent a whole day in trying to find out what it was that was hindering the younger of them from being a greater blessing. It was only gradually they discovered that the root of the trouble was *unbelief*. He did not think it possible to live out the consecrated life. He was not assured that God was ready to give the blessing. The younger had to take a meeting, but the other said, "I will take your meeting. Go home, and come back tomorrow morning at nine o'clock." He came back the next morning, and they began to speak and pray again, and in the course of the day the young man saw what it was to trust God for the power of a life in full surrender, and received a blessing from God, and since that time he had been ten times more blessed in his work than ever before. Oh, do believe that if you are ready and willing it is possible for God to make a spiritual man of you. Only try and just get a vision of the spiritual life.

What is that vision? You know the Word speaks about two powers of life—the *flesh* and the *Spirit*: the flesh, our life under the power of sin; the Spirit, God's life coming to take the place of our life. What we need, and what the Bible tells us, is to give our whole life, with every idea of strength or power, away unto death, to become nothing, and receive the life of Christ and of the Spirit to do all for us. Do believe that that can be.

You say, "That is so high and holy and glorious, I do not think I can reach it." No, you cannot, but God will send it down to you. Your reaching up is the great danger; you cannot reach it, but if you believe that God wants in a supernatural way, according to His everlasting love, to give you down from heaven the power of the Holy Spirit, then God will do for you more than you can ask or think.

I do believe that it is possible for a man to live every day as led by the Holy Ghost. I have read in God's Word that God sheds abroad His love in the heart by the Holy Spirit. I have read in God's Word that as many as are led by the Spirit, they are the children of God. I have read in God's Word that if we are born again, we are to walk by the Spirit, or in the Spirit. Dear friends, it *is* possible; it is the life God call us to, and that Christ redeemed us for. As soon as He shed His blood, He went away to heaven to send the Spirit to His people. As soon as He was glorified, His first work was to give the Holy Spirit. If you will begin to believe in the power of Christ's blood to cleanse you, and in the power of the glorified Christ to give His Spirit in your heart, you have taken the first step in the right direction.

Though you should feel ever so wretched, do hold fast to Jesus. He can fill you with the Spirit, for He has commanded you to "be filled with the Spirit."

2. But secondly, it is not enough that *a man should be really convicted of his carnality*. This is a difficult and solemn, but, as I say, needful lesson. There is a great difference—I ask you to notice this—between the sins of the unconverted man and the sins of the believer. As an unconverted man, you had to be convicted of sin, and make confession of it; you all admit that.

But what were you convicted of chiefly? Of the grossness

of sin, and very much of the guilt and punishment of sin. But there was very little conviction of inward, spiritual sins. You had no knowledge of them. There was very little conviction of inward sinfulness. God does not always give that, or ordinarily, in conversion. And so, how is a man to get rid of these two things, the more hidden sins and the deep inner sinfulness? In this way: after he has become a Christian, the Holy Spirit convicts him of the carnal, fleshly life, and then the man begins to mourn over it, and be ashamed of it, and cry out like Paul, "Oh, wretched man that I am! I am a believer, but who shall deliver me from the body of this death?" He begins to turn round for help and to ask, where am I to get deliverance? He seeks it in many ways, by struggling and resolve; but he does not get it until he is brought to cast himself absolutely at the feet of Jesus. Do not forget that if you are to become a spiritual man, if you are to be filled with the Holy Ghost, it must come from God in heaven. God alone can do it.

How different our living and praying and preaching would be, if the presence of the Holy One, who fills eternity, who fills the universe, were revealed to us! To that end, God wants to bring us to a condition of utter brokenness. Somebody said to me, "It is dreadful, that call to *die*." Yes, it is dreadful, if you had to do it in your own strength. But oh! if you would only understand that God gave Jesus to die, and that God wants to plant you into Jesus that you may be delivered from the accursed power of the flesh! Oh, do believe that it is a blessing to be utterly broken down and utterly in despair, that you may learn to trust in God alone. Paul says somewhere, in effect, "I had the sentence of death in myself, that I might learn not to trust in myself, but in God, who raised the dead." That is the place you must come to under conviction of your carnality. "The flesh prevails and triumphs in me, and I cannot conquer it. Have mercy, my God! God help me!" And God *will*. Oh, become willing to bow before God in conviction and confession.

3. And then comes the third thing and that is, to *believe that we can pass from the carnal to the spiritual condition in one moment of time*. People want to *grow out* of the carnal into the spiritual, and they never can. They seek more preaching and teaching, in order, as they think, to grow out of the carnal into the spiritual. That child that I spoke of, though ten years old, remained as a babe of six months; it had got disease, and it wanted healing. Then growth would come. Now, the carnal state is a state of terrible disease. The carnal Christian is a babe in Christ. He is a child of God, Paul says, but he has this terrible disease, and consequently he cannot grow. How is the healing to come?

It must come through God and God longs to give it you this very hour.

Let me say here that a man who becomes *a spiritual man* tonight is not yet *a man of spiritual maturity*. I cannot expect from a young Christian who has got the Holy Spirit in His fullness, what I can expect from a mature Christian who has been filled with Him for twenty years. There is a great deal of growth and maturity in the spiritual life. But what I speak of, when I speak of *one step*, is this: you can change your place, and, instead of standing in the *carnal* life, enter the *spiritual* life in one moment.

Note the reason why the two expressions are used. In

the carnal man there is something of the spiritual nature; but you know that bodies get their names from that which is their most prominent element. A thing may be used for two or three objects, but it will likely get its name from that which is the most prominent. A thing may have several characteristics, but the name will be given according to that which is the most striking.

So, Paul says in other words, to those Corinthians, "You babes in Christ are carnal; you are under the power of the flesh, giving away to temper and unloveliness, and not growing, or capable of receiving spiritual truth, with all your gifts."

And the spiritual man is a man who has not reached final perfection; there is abundant room for growth. But if you look at him, the chief mark of his nature and conduct is, that he is a *man given up to the Spirit of God*. He is not perfect, but he is a man who has taken the right position, and said, "Lord God, I have given myself to be led by Thy Spirit. Thou hast accepted me and blessed me, and the Holy Spirit now leads me."

Do let us get hold of the thought that, God helping us, we can tonight leave our place on the one side, and take it on the other.

You may have heard the story that is often used in evangelistic services, about the man who was converted by a minister drawing a line, and talking to him about it. There was a sick man, seventy years of age, and a minister visited him faithfully, and talked to him about the blood of Christ. "Oh yes," responded the man, "I know about the blood of Christ, that it can save us, and about pardon, and that if God does not pardon us we cannot enter heaven."

Yet the minister saw that the man had not the slightest sense of sin. Whatever the minister said, he said "Yes" to, but there was no life in it, no conviction of sin.

The minister tells that when he himself was beginning to get into despair, he one day prayed, "O God, help me to show this man his state." All at once a thought came into his mind. The floor of the man's room was strewn with sand, and the minister drew a line with his stick in the sand, and on the one side he wrote the words, "Sin," "Death," "Hell," and on the other side, "Christ," "Life," "Heaven."

The old man asked, "What are you doing?"

The minister answered: "Listen! Do you think one of these letters on the left side could get up and go over the line to the right side?"

"Of course not," was the answer.

Then the minister said solemnly, "Just as little can a sinner who is on the left side get over to the right side. That line divides all mankind, and those who are saved are on the right side, and the unsaved are on the left side. It is Christ who must take you up from the left side and bring you to the right side. On what side are you?" There was no answer. The minister prayed with him, and went home praying that God would bless him. He went back next day, and the question was, "Well, my friend, on what side are you?" He at once answered with a sigh, "On the wrong side." But it was not long before that man welcomed the gospel and accepted Christ.

I would like tonight to draw a line straight through the centre of this hall, and ask all of you who believe and confess that God has given you His Holy Spirit to lead you, and who know what the joy of the Holy Ghost is, to take your place at the right hand side. Then I would ask all you who have felt tonight that you are still carnal, to come to the left side and say: O God, I must confess that my Christian life is for the most part carnal, under the power of the flesh. Then I would plead with you, and tell you that you cannot save yourselves from the flesh, or get rid of it, but that if you come and accept Christ after tonight, Christ can lift you over into the new life. You belong to Christ, and He belongs to you; but what you need is just to cast ourselves upon Him, and He will reveal the power of His crucifixion in you, to give you victory over the flesh. Cast yourselves; with the confession of sin, and with utter helplessness, at the feet of the Lamb of God. He can give you deliverance.

That brings me to my last thought.

1. The first was, *a man must see the spiritual life.*

2. The second, *a man must be convicted of and confess his carnal state.*

3. The third, *a man must see that it is but one step from the one to the other*; and then, lastly;

4. *He must take the decisive step in the faith that Christ is able to keep him.* Yes, it is not a mere view, it is not a consecration in any sense of its being in our power, it is not a surrender by the strength of our will. No. These are elements that may be present, but the great thing is, that we must look to Christ to keep us tomorrow, and next day, and always; we must get the life of God within us. We want a life that will last not only till another "Keswick," but till death. We want, by the grace of God, to experience what the almighty indwelling and saving power of Christ

can do, and all that God can do for us.

Oh, God is waiting, Christ is waiting, the Holy Spirit is waiting. Do not you see what has been wrong, and why it is you have been wandering in the wilderness? Do not you see the good land, the land of promise, in which God is going to keep and bless you? Oh, remember the story of Caleb and Joshua and the spies. Ten men said in effect: We never can conquer those people. Two said: We are able, for God has promised. Step out tonight upon the promises of God. Listen to God's Word: "The law of the Spirit of Life in Christ Jesus hath made me free from the law of sin and death." Take a word like that, and claim that God shall do for you through His Holy Spirit what He has offered you.

Come tonight, and never mind though there be no new experience, and no feeling, and no excitement, and no light, but apparently darkness. Come and stand upon the Word of God, the everlasting God. God promises, as Father, His Holy Spirit to every hungering child. Will He then not give it to you? How shall He not give the Holy Spirit to them that ask Him? How could He not do it? Brethren, as truly as Christ was given for you on Calvary, and you have believed in the blood, so truly the Holy Spirit has been given for you and me. Open your hearts and be "filled with the Spirit." Come and trust the blood of Christ for the cleansing, confess the carnality of every sin, and cast it into the fountain of the blood, and then believe in the living Christ to bless you with the blessing of His Spirit.

4

"That God May Be All in All"

"Then cometh the end, when He shall have delivered up the Kingdom to God, even the Father; when He shall have put down all rule, and all authority and power. For He must reign till He hath put all enemies under His feet. The last enemy that shall be destroyed is death. For He hath put all things under His feet. But when He saith, All things are put under Him, it is manifest that He is excepted which did put all things under Him. And when all things shall be subdued unto Him, then shall the Son also Himself be subjected unto Him that put all things under Him, THAT GOD MAY BE ALL IN ALL." 1 Corinthians 15:24–28.

These last words are my text. What a mystery there is in the context! We are accustomed to speak of the two great acts of humiliation on the part of the Lord Jesus— His descending from the throne and becoming Man upon earth, a Servant among men; and of His descent, through the Cross, into the grave, the depth of humiliation under the curse. But oh! what a mystery there is here that there is a time coming in the everlasting glory when the Son of Man Himself shall be subjected unto the Father, and shall give the Kingdom into the Father's hands, and "God shall be all in all."

I cannot understand this; it passes knowledge. But I worship Christ in the glory of His subjection to the Father. And here I learn one precious lesson, and that is what I want to point you to—*that the whole aim of Christ's coming, and the whole aim of redemption, and the whole aim of Christ's work in our heart is summed up in that one thought—"That God may be all in all."*

If that is true, of what infinite consequence it is that you and I, should take the thought as our life-motto, and live it out. If we do not know that this is Christ's object, we never can understand what He expects of us, and will work in us. But if we realize where it is all tending to, that everything must be subordinated to that. Then we have a principle to rule our life, which was the very principle of the life of Christ. Let us meditate for a little while upon it, with the earnest prayer: O God, we hope to be present on that wondrous day, when Christ shall give up the Kingdom, and when the only true God of the New Testament, shall be all in all. We hope to be there to see it, and to experience it, and to rejoice in it throughout eternity. O God, give us to know something of it here, this very night.

Lord God, do take Thy place, the place Thou hast a right to take, and reveal Thy glory, that every heart may be bowed in the dust, and have but one song and one hope— *"that God may be all in all."* O God, hear us, and may every heart be subjected to Thee tonight in full reality. Amen.

I said that this is what Jesus came into the world for. This is the object of redemption. This is what we must try to understand. I want to point you to two thoughts: *First, see how Christ, in His own life, realized and worked out this—"that God may be all in all." Second, see how we, in our lives, can realize it too.*

If you look at the life of the Lord Jesus, then, you see there are five great steps in it. An old author uses the very significant expression, "The process of Jesus Christ." There is, first, *His birth*, then *His life*, and *His death*, and *His resurrection*, and *His ascension*. *In all* these things you will see how God is *all*.

Look at *His birth*. He received His life from God. It was by an act of God's omnipotence that He was born of the Virgin Mary. It was from God that He had His mission, and He continually spoke of Himself as being sent from God. Christ had His life from the Father, and He ever acknowledged it. And it is the first thing that a Christian must learn from Christ. We do not want to look at our conversion and say: I did this, and I did that, and, perhaps, to put between, God did that for me. But we want to take time in God's presence to say: As truly as it was the work of Almighty God to give His Son here upon earth, through the virgin Mary, His life in human flesh, so truly and really has God given His life into my heart. We have our life from God.

Look at the next step. *The life Christ had, as man, to maintain, He had to maintain it in the power that God gave Him*. How did He do it? He tells us: "I can do nothing of Myself." He tells us that He did not speak one word till the Father had told Him. He just lived every moment of the day with this one thought: God is absolutely all, and I am a vessel in which God reveals His glory. That was the life of Christ—entire, unbroken, continuous dependence upon God; and God really was, in His life, every hour, *all in all*. That was what Christ came to prove.

And notice that this was what man was created for—to be a vessel into which God could pour His wisdom and goodness and beauty and power. That is the nobility of the Christian. It is God that makes Seraphim and Cherubim flames of fire. The glory of God passes through them, and they have nothing in themselves. They are just vessels prepared by God, come from God, that they might let God's glory shine through them.

And so it was with the Son. Sin came in, the terrible sin, first, of the fallen angels, and then of man. They exalted themselves against God, and would not receive the glory of God, and they fell into the "outer darkness"; first the devils, and then man. And Christ came to restore man, and so Christ lived among us, and day by day He just depended upon the Father for everything. Notice, He would not touch a bit of bread until the Father gave it to Him. He had the power, and He was very hungry, but He would not make a stone into bread, though He could have done it, until the Father said: My son, eat this. Christ lived a life of absolute dependence upon God, waiting for God day and night; and that is the Man who is one day, in glory, to effect it that God shall be *all in all*.

Then, next, He not only received His life from God, and lived it in dependence on God, but He gave it up to God. He did it in obedience. What is obedience? Giving up my will to the will of another. When a soldier bows to his general, or a scholar to his teacher, he gives up his will—and my will is my life—he gives up himself to the rule and mastery and the power of another. And Christ did that. "I came not to do Mine own will"; "Lo, I come to do Thy will." In Gethsemane He said, "Not my will but Thine be done." Then He went further, and on the Cross He carried out what had been settled in Gethsemane, and gave up His life to God, and He thereby taught us that the only thing that life is worth living for is *to give it back to God even unto death*. If you take your life and spend it on yourself, even partly, you are abusing it, you are taking it away from its noblest use. O Christian, learn from Christ that the beauty of having life and will and body is, that you can give it to God, and that then God will fill it with His glory. Yes, the Lord Jesus came and gave up His life unto the very death.

We have been talking about crucifixion and death more than once during these days. Just let me say this in passing we must not always look at crucifixion and death as necessary only from the side of sin. That is only half the truth—the negative side. But we must look at it on the other side, the side of the Lord Jesus. Why did He give up that life unto death, and what did He get by it? He gave up His earthly life, and God gave Him a heavenly life. He gave up the life of humiliation, and God gave Him a life of fellowship and glory. Christian, do you want a life of fellowship with God, and of glory and power and joy, even here upon earth? Remember, then, that there is but one way to secure it. Give your life up to God. That is the one way. That is what Christ did. He gave up His life unto the very death, into the hands of God. Oh do not you see that in the life of Christ, God was everything, God "all in all"? Christ worked it out, and proved most gloriously that God can be, and God must be, "all in all."

Take the next step; *He was raised again from the dead*. What does the Resurrection mean? If you want to understand that, ask first, what does the Cross mean? Jesus parted with His life, and what does that say to us? He gave Himself up into utter helplessness to wait upon God, to see what God would do. He said: I cannot seize the heavenly life for Myself; I wait till my Father gives it to me. The grave was His humiliation. "My flesh shall rest in hope." There he waited, until God the Father raised Him up in everlasting glory. The time of Jesus in the grave was a very short time—only a portion of three days; but it teaches us the one lesson we need to learn from Jesus, the lesson of the entire giving up of our life into God's hands, to let God do all in us, to let God be "all in all." Give up yourself in utter dependence upon God, unto death. Lose everything, and God will raise you up in glory. Christ could never have ascended to sit upon the throne, never could have accomplished His work of preparing the kingdom that He could give to the Father, if He had not begun by giving up *Himself*, and let God do all.

And it was even so, too, with His ascension to heaven, and His entering into glory. Well, then, the five steps we have been considering are these: 1. Christ had His life from God; 2. He lived it in dependence upon God; 3. He gave it up in death to God; 4. He received in the Resurrection from God; and 5. He ascended to God, and was glorified in it with God forever.

Remember that the throne in heaven is not the throne of the Lamb of God alone; it is the throne of God and the Lamb. Jesus went to share the throne with the Father; the Father was always first, and Jesus second. Even on the throne of heaven our glorified Lord Jesus honours the Father as Father, and honours God as God. It is a deep mystery, but it is the blessed subordination of the Son to the Father. Let us meditate until our souls get full of the thought and the blessed truth: the one thing that God must have He gets, even from His own Son—subordination, subjection; and it is because Christ sits in this spirit on the throne of glory, that one day He can give up the kingdom to the Father.

Let us now take in this—which I said was my first great thought. The Lord Jesus came to remove the terrible curse that sin had wrought, the terrible ruin that had come by man's pride and self-exaltation; and He came to live out, during thirty-three years, *that God must be all in all*.

And let me ask, in passing, did God disappoint Him? I tell you, no. God lifted Him to the throne of the everlasting glory, and to equality on the throne with Himself, because He had humbled Himself to honour His God. And if we want God to bless us, it is down in the place of dependence and humility that the blessing will be found.

But now we come to the *second* thought, and it is this: *Are we called to live, just as much as Christ did, that God may be all in all?* Is there any greater obligation on Christ to let God be *all in all* than on us? Most people think so, but the Bible does not. The obligation ought to be greater on us, for He is the Son of the Father, and God with God; but we are creatures of the dust. Oh, there can be no thought of our existence having been given for anything but just for the blessed object that God may be "all in all," in us and to us. Have we understood that, and have we expected it, and have we sought for it, and have we ever learned to say with Christ: It is worth giving up everything that God may have His place and be *"all in all"*?

But how can we attain to such a life? All our teaching about consecration will be vain, unless it come to that—God must be *all*. What is the meaning of our talking about giving ourselves as a living sacrifice? It cannot be, unless it is actually true that in our life God is *all*. What is the reason of so much complaint of feebleness, of failure, of lost blessing, of walking in the dark? It is nothing but this: God does not get His place amongst us. I do not say that of the unsanctified, and half sanctified, but I say of the best among us. God does not get His place. And I ask you tonight, O saints of God, to pray with your whole heart, that God would take His place in the life of every one of us, and that the inconceivable majesty of God and His claim upon us may be so revealed that we shall sink as atoms in the dust, and say: God, be Thou all, and take all, and have all. God help us to do so.

Now, what are the steps by which the soul can be brought, in some measure, to live like Christ every day, so that God may be *"all in all"*?

My answer is first of all, *Take time and trouble to give God His place*. Study your God, meditate more upon your God than you have done, and try to find out what is the place that God desires to take. Do not be content with the sort of vague conception: Yes, of course there is the throne in the heaven, and God is there. For remember, God is not only an outward Being, so to speak. There is a locality and a throne where the glory of God is specially revealed; but God has an inward being. He dwells even in nature, and how much more in the heart of His redeemed ones and saints! I want to get some conception of what is the place of God, and words can hardly tell. I can only say this: God is the fountain of all life. Every bit of life in the universe is the work of God. If you really give God His place, then you will get, oh, such a humbling conviction that there is nothing but what must come from God; that God fills all things. The Bible says He works all in all, and so you will begin to say: If God is everywhere and in everything, I ought to see Him in nature, and in providence, and in everything; I ought always to be seeing my God. The believer can come to that; when he sees God everywhere, he begins to give God His place. He cannot rise in the mourning without giving God His place, and saying: Lord God, Thou glorious Being, Thou art "all in all." He begins to say to his fellow-believers: My brothers, I am afraid that in our prayer-meetings we do not let God take His place. We pray because we have a God to pray to, and we know something about God; but how little we in our souls realize the everlasting God! In our little prayer-meetings the everlasting God of heaven is present, and if He gets His place He will take charge of the meetings, and He will give blessing, and He will work by His mighty power.

Oh, just think of it! Take our chairman for this our meeting, for instance. He guides our meeting, he calls on one to pray, and another to speak; he tells us what to sing, and gives orders what is to be done. He has a little kingdom in this tent, and he manages it, and you are grateful for it. But God!—people do not allow Him to manage the Church service, Christian Convention, or the prayer-meeting. Do not we thank God for every earthly gift? But oh that we might each learn to understand, in the church every day, in the prayer-meeting, in the closet: I must give time to let my God take His place.

Will God do it? God is waiting to do it. *God longs to do it.* And then, not only in the closet and the prayer-meeting, and the Christian Convention and the church, but just as one of you takes the place of master or mistress in your house, and you sit at the head of the table, and you order the servant, and you manage everything, so God is willing in my heart and in yours to take the place of Master and of God. Brethren, have we given this glorious God the place He ought to have? Let us in our heart say, No. And God forgive us if *we* have taken the place that Christ's redemption has given Him, and that Christ wants to give Him in us. Let us come tonight, ere we part, and say: God shall have His place.

I might speak still further, in this connection, of the Church of Christ. Has God His place there? Alas! No. May God humble us and stir in us an unquenchable longing, "that God may be all in all."

That is my first lesson: *Give God His place*; but take time and take trouble to do it. Take heed and be quiet. The prophet says: "Be silent all flesh before the Lord." Let the flesh be kept down. Wait, and give God time to reveal Himself.

The second answer to the question, *How am I* in my life to attain this, "That God may be all in all," and to work it out and prove it? Is, *Accept God's will in everything*.

Where do I find God's will? I find God's will in His Word. I have often heard it said that people have said, "I believe every word within these two covers has come from God"; and I have sometimes heard it said, "I want to believe every promise between these two covers"; but I have not often heard it said, "I accept every commandment within these two covers." But let us say it. If you like, write in the front page of your Bible what I once wrote in the front page of a young man's: "Every promise of God in this book I desire to believe, every command of God in this book I desire to accept." That is one step in the way to let God be "all in all." Give up your life to be the embodiment and expression and incarnation of the will of God.

Then, further, *accept the will of God, not only in the Bible, but also in providence.* I find thousands of Christians who have never learned that lesson. Do you know what that means? When Joseph's brethren sold him, he accepted God's hand in that, and it is written that when he went to Potiphar as a slave, "God was with him." He was not parted from God when he had to part from his home. I read of David that when Shimei cursed him, he said, in effect: That is God. He saw God in that; he met God there in that cursing of Shimei, because God allowed it. When Judas came to kiss Christ and betray Him, and when the soldiers bound Him, and when Peter denied Him, and when Caiaphas condemned Him, and when Pilate gave Him over, Christ saw God in everything. So Christ could drink the cup, for He saw the hand of the Father holding it.

Oh, let us learn, in every trial, in every trouble, great and little, to see God at once. Meet your God there, and let God be "all in all." There does not a hair of your head fall without the will of your Father. Meet the will of your Father in every trial, in the deepest trial and the heaviest;

the Son of God walks there. And in the smallest trials—the servant who torments you, the child who hinders you, the friend who has hurt you by neglect, the enemy who has reproached you, who has spoken evil of you and robbed you of your good name, the difficulty that worries you— oh! Why do not you say: It is my God who comes to me in every difficulty. I will meet Him, and honour Him, and give myself to Him; and may He keep me!

There are two great privileges in meeting God in a difficulty, and knowing Him. The first is that, even though the difficulty come through my own fault, if I confess it, then I can say: God has allowed me to come into this fault, to come into this difficulty, in order to teach me a lesson. My God allowed me to come into it, and He must teach me to glorify Him in it. If a father takes his child to a distant place to school, the child trusts the father to provide for him there. It is not willingly that the father sends the child away from under his eyes. And if God brings you into a difficulty by an act of your own, then you can count upon it that God will give you grace to be humble and patient, and be perfected through the suffering and chastisement, that in everything He may take His place. You will be able to look to Him with double confidence when you can say: It is Thou who hast brought me here, and not man, and Thou alone canst take me out of it. Oh! If you would only allow God to be "all in all" in every providence, what a blessed life you would be living! Nothing can separate you from the love of God in Christ Jesus. You have a wonderful place provided for you in His love. Oh! Learn to take this as the key out of every difficulty—*God is all in all*. And in prayer, day by day, make it your earnest supplication that God may be all.

Then the third point. The first was, give God His place; the second, accept His will. The third is, *Trust His almighty power*. Trust Him every day. I wish I could tell you rightly what I see a glimpse of, and that is that the whole of our Christian life every day is to be the work of God Himself. Paul speaks of it so often. "It is God that worketh in you both to will and to do." The will and the desire to obey— that is God's work in you, and that is only half of it. But He will work *to do*, as well as to *will*, if you will own Him practically in your life as *all*. In Hebrews we read: "The God of peace… make you perfect in every good work to do His will, working in you that which is well-pleasing in His sight, through Jesus Christ." Here is my watch. Now, as surely as the watchmaker has made that watch, and worked at it, and cut it, and cleaned it, and polished it, and put in every little wheel and every little spring, just so the living God is actually and actively engaged in the work of perfecting your life every moment. God is willing to work in our meeting from half-past six to half-past eight, every moment. And why does not He work more powerfully? Simply because you do not yield to His power, you do not fully give Him His place, you do not wait upon Him to do it. Tell Him: My God, here I am now. I give Thee Thy right place.

Suppose a canvas could move about, and that when a painter came into his studio to paint an unfinished picture, it always removed to some other part of the room, of course the painter could not paint. But suppose the canvas began to say: O painter, I will be still; come and do thy work and paint thy beautiful picture. Then the painter would come and do it. And if you say to God: Thou art the mighty Workman, the wondrous Artist. I am still. Here I am. I trust Thy power, ah, believe it, God will then work wonders with you. God never works anything but wonders. That is His nature, even in what we call the laws of nature. Take the simplest thing, a blade of grass, or a little worm, or a flower; what wonders men of science tell us about them. And will not God work wonders in my heart and yours? He will. And why does not He do it more? Because we do not let Him. Oh learn, to give Him His place, to accept His will, and then to trust His mighty work.

In Thy strength I lay me down,
    Clay within the Potter's hands,
Moulded by Thy gentle will,
    Mightier than all commands:
Moved and shaped by Thee alone,
Now and evermore Thine own.

Is that true of you? God is willing to mould you as really as the potter moulds his clay. He will do it. Let us believe it, and trust His mighty power, and let us trust His power especially to do things above our conception, or above what we could ask or think. *God is waiting to do for you more than you can even conceive.* Every yearning of your heart, every message that you have heard, of which you have said: I wish I had that; every prayer you have sent up. Oh, just believe that God is willing to work it all in you, and that He is waiting to do it; that in every difficulty, in every circumstance, God is there to work in you. Trust in Him and honour Him, and let Him be "all in all."

And then, once again, if you would honour God, *sacrifice everything for His kingdom and glory*. If God is to be all in all, it must not be so much, I must be happy, and I must be holy, and I must have God's approval. No. The root principle of Christ's life was self-sacrifice unto God for man. That is what He came for, and it is a principle that every redeemed soul carries within him as unquenchable; but alas! it can be smothered. But understand that your God longs to rule the world, and your Christ is upon the throne, leading you on as His soldiers, and wanting to bless you with victory upon victory. Have you given yourselves up to God's glory? Alas, alas!

The soldier upon earth says: Anything for my king and country, anything when my general leads me on to victory. My home I leave, and my comforts. I give my life. And are earthly kings to have such devotion, and you and I merely *talk* about the glory of God and His being "all in all," when there is a call that we should help to prepare the kingdom for Christ to give up to the Father, and when Christ tells us He is waiting for our help and depending upon it?

Shall we not each say, God must be "all in all"; I will sacrifice everything for Him? May God help us tonight to make a consecration afresh of our whole being to the furtherance of Christ's kingdom. And whether it be in mission work far away, or in Christian work near at home, or whether it be that as yet we do not know how to work,—whatever it be, let everyone yield himself a willing sacrifice, and then the very weakest Christ can and will use for the glory of God.

If you want to take a word as your motto and watchword, let it be, Sacrifice everything and anything for the glory of your God. And if you do not know what to sacrifice, ask Him. Be honest, be earnest, be simple, be childlike, and say: Lord, every penny I have is Thine, and every comfort is thine. If Thou needest it for Thy kingdom, I offer it to Thee. Oh, in eternity, will a man grudge having made himself poor for the bringing about of that majestic spectacle, when the Son shall say, in a new sense, "It is finished," and give the kingdom to the Father, "that God may be all in all"? Do you hope to be there? Do you hope to have a share in the glory of that august scene, and are you unwilling tonight to say: Anything that I can do for that glory, Lord, here I am? Give yourself up to Him.

And now the last thought, and that is, *Wait on God*.

I have been speaking, and you have been thinking about God; that is one thing. But oh, to know God in His glory within our souls, that is another thing. I told you what you ought to do; that you ought to meditate and study, and try to form a right conception of the place God should occupy in your life. But that is not enough. You must do something else. I said: Give yourselves up to the will of God, prove the power of God, and seek the glory of God throughout the earth. But the chief thing is... wait upon God.

And why must we do that? Because it is only God who can reveal Himself. Remember that when God came to Adam, or Noah, or Abraham, or Moses, it was God who came forth out of heaven and met them, and showed Himself in some form or other. That was under the old dispensation. And it depends today on the good pleasure of God to reveal Himself. Not an arbitrary good pleasure. No. It all depends upon whether He has found a heart hungering for Him. Oh that God would give us that hunger, and teach us to cry like David, "My soul thirsteth for God!" Wait upon God. Make that in your closet a part of your life more and more systematically. Do not be afraid if people say, Do you want to make Quakers of us? Let us remember that every portion of Christ's body has got a lesson for us. I do not think one of you will suffer if you learn the lesson in your closet of keeping silence before God, just with one prayer: Lord God, reveal Thyself in the depths of my heart. And though you do not expect a vision, though you do not get a manifestation—that is not what *should* be sought; it is that the soul should open itself to God, and wait upon Him that He may come in. "Verily, Thou art a God that hidest Thyself." You cannot see Him always, but He will come in and take possession of you, if you are ready for His incoming, and will reveal Himself, and work mightily in you.

Wait upon God. In your prayer-meetings let that be the first thing. It is the mischief of our prayer in our closets and prayer-meetings, that we begin to pray at once as if all was right. "Oh yes," we say, "God will do it"; and we do not take trouble to let our souls worship in holy awe and reverence and childlike trust. We do not take time to say: Father, let it please Thee to come near, and to meet me. Some have said, Oh! if we could have more time for waiting upon God!" I think so too. I am a stranger. I do not want to be presumptuous, or to take unwarrantable liberty; but I do want to say that if next year it were so ordered that you could get that new hall, so that those people who wished it could go there to wait upon God in prayer, others being at liberty to go elsewhere to hear the speakers if they so desired, then I believe the result would be one of wonderful blessing.

The responsibility resting upon this body of believers is tremendous. We confess that many of us have got a secret which other Christians have not got. We do not judge, but we confess that God has taught us something wonderful. Let us confess it boldly. But then, if that is true, we must get still nearer God, and have more of God, in order to teach other Christians how they can find God. You cannot find God without waiting upon Him. "Wait, I say, on the Lord." These are the steps by which we can come to have it in our hearts and lives: God is all in all; the steps by which we can be prepared for taking our place in that glorious company who shall be present at that august, magnificent scene, when Christ shall give up the kingdom to the Father, "*that God may be* ALL IN ALL."

5

Separated Unto the Holy Ghost

"Now there were in the church that was at Antioch certain prophets and teachers; as Barnabas, and Simeon that was called Niger, and Lucius of Cyrene, and Manaen... and Saul. As they ministered to the Lord and fasted, the Holy Ghost said, Separate Me Barnabas and Saul for the work whereunto I have called them. And when they had fasted and prayed, and laid their hands on them, they sent them away. So they, being sent forth by the Holy Ghost, departed unto Seleucia." Acts 13:1–4

We are met here to know the will of our God concerning His work, and to seek from Him the power for it. In the story of our text we shall find some precious thoughts to guide us as to what God would have of us, and what God would do for us.

The great lesson of the verses I read is this: *That the Holy Ghost is the director of the work of God upon the earth.* And what we want to do if we are to work rightly for God, and if God is to bless our work, is to see that we stand in a right relation to the Holy Ghost, that we give Him every day the place of honour that belongs to Him, and that in all our work and, what is more, in all our private inner life, the Holy Ghost shall always have the first place. Let me point out to you some of the precious thoughts our passage suggests.

1. And, first of all, we see that *God has His own plans with regard to His kingdom*. His Church at Antioch had been established. God had certain plans and intentions with regard to Asia, and with regard to Europe. He had conceived them; they were His, and He made them known to His servants. We talk about the winter campaign in the East End; but do we not all know that our great Commander organizes the campaign, and that His generals and officers do not always know the great plans? They often receive sealed orders, and they have to wait on Him for what He gives them as orders. God in heaven has planned for East London; we cannot doubt it. God in heaven has wishes, and a will, in regard to the work that ought to be done, and to the way in which it has to be done. Blessed is the man who gets into God's secrets and works under God.

Some years ago, at Wellington, where I live, we opened a Mission Institute, what is counted there a fine large building. At our opening services the Principal said something that I have never forgotten. He remarked: "Last year we gathered here to lay the foundation stone, and what was there then to be seen? Nothing but rubbish, and stones, and bricks, and the ruins of an old building that had been pulled down.

"There we laid the foundation-stone, and very few knew what the building was that was to rise. No one knew it perfectly in every detail except one man, the architect. In his mind it was all clear, and as the contractor and the mason and the carpenter came to their work they took their orders from him, and the humblest labourer had to be obedient to orders, and the structure rose, and this beautiful building has been completed. And just so," he added, "this building that we open today is but laying the foundation of a work of which only God knows what it is to become." But God has His workers and His plans clearly mapped out, and our position is to wait, that God should communicate to us as much of His will as each time is needful.

We have simply to be faithful in obedience, carrying out His orders. God has a plan for His Church upon earth and for His Church in London. But alas! we too often make our plan, and we think that we know what ought to be done. We ask God first to bless our feeble efforts, instead of absolutely refusing to go unless God go before us. God has planned for the work and the extension of His kingdom. The Holy Ghost has had that work given in charge to Him. "The work whereunto I have called them." The work in East London is Holy Ghost work. May God therefore help us all to be afraid of touching "the ark of God" except as we are led by the Holy Ghost.

2. Then the *second* thought. *God is willing and able to reveal to His servants what His will is*. Yes, blessed be God, communications come down from heaven still. As we read here what the Holy Ghost said, so still the Holy Ghost will speak to His Church and His people. In these later days He has often done it; He has come to individual men, and by His divine teaching He has led them out into fields of labour that others could not at first understand or approve; into ways and methods that did not recommend themselves to the majority. But the Holy Ghost does still in our time teach His people. Thank God, in our missionary

societies and in our home missions, and in a thousand forms of work, the guiding of the Holy Ghost is known, but we are all ready, I think, to confess too *little* known. We have not learned enough to wait upon Him, and so we want to make our Convention a solemn declaration before God: O God, we want to wait more for Thee to show us Thy will.

Do not ask God only for power. Many a Christian has his own plan of working, but God must send the power. The man works in his own will, and God must give the grace—the one reason why God gives so little grace often and so little success. But let us all take our place before God and say: What is done in the will of God, the strength of God will not be withheld from it; what is done in the will of God must have the mighty blessing of God. And so let our first desire be to have the will of God revealed. If you ask me, Is it an easy thing to get these communications from heaven, and to understand them? I can give you the answer. It is easy to those who are in right fellowship with heaven, and who understand the art of waiting upon God. How often we ask, How can a person know the will of God? And people want, when they are in perplexity, to pray very earnestly that God should answer them at once. But God can only reveal His will to a heart that is humble and tender and empty.

God can only reveal His will in perplexities and special difficulties to a heart that has learned to obey and honour Him loyally in little things and in daily life.

3. That brings me to the *third* thought. *Note the disposition to which the Spirit reveals God's will*. What do we read here? There were a number of men ministering to

the Lord and fasting, and the Holy Ghost came and spoke to them. Some people understand this passage very much as they would in reference to a missionary committee of our day. We see there is an open field, and we have had our missions in other fields, and we are going to get on to that field. We have virtually settled that, and we pray about it. But the position was a very different one in those former days. I doubt whether any of them thought of Europe, for later on even Paul himself essayed to go back into Asia, till the night vision called him by the will of God. Look at those men. God had done wonders; He had extended the Church to Antioch, and He had given rich and large blessing.

Now, here are these men ministering to the Lord, serving Him with prayer and fasting. What a deep conviction they have it must all come direct from heaven. We are in fellowship with the risen Lord; we must have close union with him, and somehow He will let us know what He wants. And there they were, empty, ignorant, helpless, glad and joyful, but deeply humbled. O Lord, they seem to say, we are Thy servants, and in fasting and prayer we wait upon Thee. What is Thy will for us?

Was it not the same with Peter? He was on the housetop, fasting and praying, and little did he think of the vision and the command to go to Caesarea. He was ignorant of what his work might be. May God grant that this may become our position, and may we all realize that it is in hearts entirely surrendered to the Lord Jesus, in hearts separating themselves from the world, and even from ordinary religious exercises, and giving themselves up in intense prayer to look to their Lord—it is in such hearts that the heavenly will of God will be made manifest.

You know that word: "fasting" occurs a second time (in the third verse), "They fasted and prayed." When you pray, you love to go into your closet, according to the command of Jesus, and shut the door. You shut out business and company and pleasure and anything that can distract, and you want to be alone with God. But in one shape even the material world follows you there. You must eat. These men wanted to shut themselves out from the influences of the material and the visible, and they fasted. What they ate was simply enough to supply the wants of nature, and in the intensity of their souls they thought to give expression to their letting go of everything on earth, in their fasting before God. Oh, may God give us that intensity of desire, that separation from everything, because we want to wait upon God, that the Holy Ghost may reveal to us God's blessed will.

4. The *fourth* thought. What is now the will of God as the Holy Ghost reveals it? It is contained in one word: *Separation unto the Holy Ghost*. That is the keynote of the message from heaven. "Separate Me Barnabas and Saul for the work whereunto I have called them." The work is Mine and I care for it, and I have chosen these men and called them, and I want you who represent the Church of Christ upon earth, to set them apart unto Me.

Look at this heavenly message in its two-fold aspect. The men were to be *set apart* to the Holy Ghost, and *the Church was to do this separating work*. The Holy Ghost could trust these men to do it in a right spirit. There they were abiding in fellowship with the heavenly, and the Holy Ghost could say to them, Do you the work of

separating these men. And these were the men the Holy
Ghost had prepared, and He could say of them, Let them
be separated unto Me.

Here we come to the very root, to the very life of our
need as workers. The question is amongst us, What is
needed that the power of God should rest upon us more
mightily, that the blessing of God should be poured out
more abundantly among those poor wretched people
and perishing sinners among whom we labour? And the
answer from heaven is, I want men separated unto the
Holy Ghost. What does that imply? You know that there
are two spirits on earth. Christ said, when He spoke about
the Holy Spirit, "The world cannot receive Him." Paul
said, "We have received not the spirit of the world, but
the Spirit that is of God." That is the great want in every
worker—the spirit of the world going out, and the Spirit
of God coming in to take possession of the inner life, and
of the whole being.

I am sure there are workers who often cry to God for
the Holy Spirit to come upon them as a Spirit of power
for their work, and when they feel that measure of power,
and get blessing, they thank God for it. But God wants
something more and something higher. God wants us to
seek for the Holy Spirit as a Spirit of power in our own
heart and life, to conquer self and cast out sin, and work
the blessed and beautiful image of Jesus into us.

There is a difference between the power of the Spirit as
a gift, and the power of the Spirit for the grace of a holy
life. A man may often have a measure of the power of the
Spirit, but if there be not a large measure of the Spirit as the
Spirit of grace and of holiness, the defect will be manifest

in his work. He may be made the means of conversion, but he never will help people on to a higher standard of spiritual life, and when he passes away a great deal of his work may pass away too. But a man who is separated unto the Holy Ghost is a man who is given up to say: Father, let the Holy Ghost have full dominion over me, in my home, in my temper, in every word of my tongue, in every thought of my heart, in every feeling towards my fellowmen; let the Holy Spirit have entire possession. Is that what has been the longing and the covenant of your heart with your God to be a man or a woman separated and given up unto the Holy Ghost? I pray you listen to the voice of heaven. "Separate Me," said the Holy Ghost. Yes, *separated* unto the Holy Ghost.

May God grant that the Word may enter into the very depths of our being to search us, and if we discover that we have not come out from the world entirely, if God discovers to us that the self-life, self-will, self-exaltation are there, let us humble ourselves before Him.

We have announced that these are to be days of humiliation; and when once we are fairly started in our work we want to take time to humble ourselves before God, and to ask God Himself to humble us under His mighty hand. Man, woman, brother, sister, you are a worker separated unto the Holy Ghost. Is that true? Has that been your longing desire? Has that been your surrender? Has that been what you have expected through faith in the power of our risen and almighty Lord Jesus? If not, here is the call of faith, and here is the key of blessing *separated unto the Holy Ghost*, God write the word in our hearts! I said the Holy Spirit spoke to that church as a church capable of doing that work. The Holy Spirit trusted them. God grant that our churches, our missionary societies, and our workers' unions, that all our directors and councils and committees may be men and women who are fit for the work of *separating workers unto the Holy Spirit*. We can ask God for that too.

5. Then comes my *fifth* thought, and it is this: *This holy partnership with the Holy Spirit in His work becomes a matter of consciousness and of action*. These men, what did they do? They set apart Paul and Barnabas, and then it is written of the two that they, being sent forth by the Holy Ghost, went down to Seleucia. Oh, what fellowship! The Holy Spirit in heaven doing part of the work, man on earth doing the other part. After the ordination of the man upon earth, it is written in God's inspired Word that they were sent forth by the Holy Ghost.

And see how this partnership calls to new prayer and fasting. They had for a certain time been ministering to the Lord and fasting, perhaps days; and the Holy Spirit speaks, and they have got to do the work and to enter into partnership, and at once they come together for more prayer and fasting. That is the spirit in which they obey the command of their Lord. And that teaches us that it is not only in the beginning of our Christian work, but all along, that we need to have our strength in prayer. If there is one thought with regard to the Church of Christ, which at times comes to me with overwhelming sorrow; if there is one thought in regard to my own life, of which I am ashamed; if there is one thought of which I feel that the Church of Christ has not accepted it and not grasped it; if there is one thought which makes me pray to God,

Oh, teach us, by Thy grace, new things it is the wonderful power that prayer is meant to have in the kingdom. We have so little availed ourselves of it.

We have all read the expression of Christian in Bunyan's great work, when he found he had the key in his breast that should unlock the dungeon. We have the key that can unlock the dungeon of heathendom. But, oh, we are far more occupied with our work than we are in prayer. We believe more in speaking to men than we believe in speaking to God. Learn from these men that the work which the Holy Ghost commands must call us to new fasting and prayer, to new separation from the spirit and the pleasures of the world, to new consecration to God and to His fellowship. Those men gave themselves up to fasting and prayer, and if in all our ordinary Christian work there were more prayer, there would be more blessing in our own inner life. If we felt and prove and testified to the world, My only strength is in keeping every minute in contact with Christ, every minute allowing God to work in me if that were our spirit, would not, by the grace of God, our lives be holier? Would not they be more abundantly fruitful?

I hardly know a more solemn warning in God's Word than that which we find in Galatians 3, where Paul asked, "Having begun in the Spirit, are ye now made perfect by the flesh?" Do you understand what that means? A terrible danger in Christian work, just as in a Christian life that is begun with much prayer, begun in the Holy Spirit, is that it may be gradually shunted off on to the lines of the flesh; and the word comes, "Having begun in the Spirit, are ye now made perfect by the flesh?" In the time of our first perplexity and helplessness we prayed much to God, and God answered and God blessed, and our organization became perfected, and our band of workers became large; but gradually the organization and the work and the rush have so got possession of us that the power of the Spirit, in which we began when we were a small company, has almost got lost. Oh, I pray you, note it well! It was with new prayer and fasting, with more prayer and fasting, that this company of disciples carried out the command of the Holy Ghost. "My soul, wait thou only upon God." That is our highest and most important work. The Holy Spirit comes in answer to believing prayer.

You know when the exalted Jesus had ascended to the throne, for ten days the footstool of the throne was the place where His waiting disciples cried to Him. And that is the law of the kingdom—the King upon the throne, the servants upon the footstool. May God find us there unceasingly.

Then comes the *last* thought. What a wonderful blessing comes when the Holy Ghost is allowed to lead and to direct the work, and when it is carried on in obedience to Him! You know the story of the mission on which Barnabas and Saul were sent out. You know what power there was with them. The Holy Ghost sent them, and they went on from place to place with large blessing. The Holy Ghost was their leader further on. You recollect how it was by the Spirit that Paul was hindered from going again into Asia, and was led away over to Europe. Oh, the blessing that rested upon that little company of men, and upon their ministry unto the Lord!

I pray you, let us learn to believe that God has a blessing

for us. The Holy Ghost, into whose hands God has put the work, has been called "the executive of the Holy Trinity." The Holy Ghost has not only power, but He has the Spirit of love. He is brooding over this dark world, and He is willing to bless. And why is there not more blessing? There can be but one answer. We have not honoured the Holy Ghost as we should have done. Is there one who can lift up his hand and say, That is not true? Is not every thoughtful heart ready to cry, God forgive me that I have not honoured the Holy Spirit as I should have done, that I have grieved Him, that I have allowed self and the flesh and my own will to work where the Holy Ghost should have been honoured? May God forgive me that I have allowed self and the flesh and the will actually to have the place that God wanted the Holy Ghost to get. Oh, the sin is greater than we know! No wonder that there is so much feebleness and failure in the Church of Christ!

6

Peter's Repentance

"And the Lord turned, and looked upon Peter. And Peter remembered the word of the Lord, how he had said unto him, Before the cock crow, thou shalt deny me thrice. And Peter went out, and wept bitterly." Luke 22:61, 62

That was the turning-point in the history of Peter. Christ had said to him: "Thou canst not follow me now." Peter was not in a fit state to follow Christ, because he had not been brought to an end of himself; he did not know himself, and he therefore could not follow Christ. But when he went out and wept bitterly, then came the great change. Christ previously said to him: "When thou art converted, strengthen thy brethren." Here is the point where Peter was converted from self to Christ.

I thank God for the story of Peter. I do not know a man in the Bible who gives us greater comfort. When we look at his character, so full of failures, and at what Christ made him by the power of the Holy Ghost, there is hope for every one of us. But remember, before Christ could fill Peter with the Holy Spirit and make a new man of him, he had to go out and weep bitterly; he had to be humbled. If we want to understand this, I think there are four points that we must look at. First, let us look at *Peter the devoted disciple of Jesus*; next, at *Peter as he lived the life of self*; then at *Peter in his repentance*; and last, at *what Christ made of Peter by the Holy Spirit*.

First, then, look at *Peter the devoted disciple of Christ*. Christ called Peter to forsake his nets, and follow Him. Peter did it at once, and he afterward could say rightly to the Lord: "We have forsaken all and followed thee." Peter was a man of *entire surrender*; he gave up all to follow Jesus. Peter was also a man of *true obedience*. You remember Christ said to him, "Launch out into the deep, and let down the net." Peter the fisherman knew there were no fish there, for they had been toiling all night and had caught nothing; but he said: "At thy word I will let down the net." He submitted to the word of Jesus. Further, he was a man of *great faith*. When he saw Christ walking on the sea, he said: "Lord, if it be thou, bid me come unto thee"; and at the voice of Christ he stepped out of the boat and walked upon the water. And Peter was a man of *spiritual insight*. When Christ asked the disciples: "Whom do ye say that I am?" Peter was able to answer: "Thou art the Christ, the Son of the living God." And Christ said: "Blessed art thou, Simon Barjona; for flesh and blood hath not revealed it unto thee, but my Father which is in heaven." And Christ spoke of him as the *rock* man, and of his having the keys of the kingdom. Peter was a splendid man, a devoted disciple of Jesus, and if he were living nowadays, everyone would say that he was an advanced Christian. And yet how much there was wanting in Peter!

Look next at *Peter living the life of self, pleasing self, and trusting self, and seeking the honour of self*. You recollect that just after Christ had said to him: "Flesh and blood hath not revealed it unto thee, but my Father which is in heaven," Christ began to speak about His sufferings, and Peter dared to say: "Be it far from thee, Lord; this shall not be unto thee." Then Christ had to say: "Get thee behind me, Satan; for thou savourest not the things that be of God, but those that be of men."

There was Peter in his self-will, trusting his own wisdom, and actually forbidding Christ to go and die. Whence did that come? Peter trusted in himself and his own thoughts about divine things. We see later on, more than once, that among the disciples there was a questioning who should be the greatest, and Peter was one of them, and he thought he had a right to the very first place. He sought his own honour even above the others. It was the life of self strong in Peter. He had left his boats and his nets, but not his old self.

When Christ had spoken to him about His sufferings, and said: "Get thee behind me, Satan," He followed it up by saying: "If any man will come after me, let him deny himself, and take up his cross, and follow me." No man can follow Him unless he do that. Self must be utterly denied. What does that mean? When Peter denied Christ, we read that he said three times: "I do not know the man"; in other words: "I have nothing to do with Him; He and I are no friends; I deny having any connection with Him." Christ told Peter that he must deny self. Self must be ignored, and it's every claim rejected. That is the root of true discipleship; but Peter did not understand it, and could not obey it. And what happened? When the last night came, Christ said to him: "Before the cock crow twice thou shalt deny me thrice." But with what self-confidence

Peter said: "Though all should forsake thee, yet will not I. I am ready to go with thee, to prison and to death." Peter meant it honestly, and Peter really intended to do it; but Peter did not know himself. He did not believe he was as bad as Jesus said he was.

We have just sung from that hymn "Nothing unclean!" And we perhaps thought of individual sins that come between us and God. But what are we to do with that self-life which is all unclean, our very nature? What are we to do with that flesh that is entirely under the power of sin? Deliverance from that is what we need. Peter knew it not, and therefore it was that in his self-confidence he went forth and denied his Lord.

Notice how Christ uses that word *deny* twice. He said to Peter the first time, *"Deny self "*; He said to Peter the second time, *"Thou wilt deny Me."* It is either of the two. There is no choice for us; we must either deny self or deny Christ. There are two great powers fighting each other—the self-nature in the power of sin, and Christ in the power of God. Either of these must rule within us.

Look now *at Peter's repentance*. Peter denied his Lord thrice, and then the Lord looked upon him; and that look of Jesus broke the heart of Peter, and all at once there opened up before him the terrible sin that he had committed, the terrible failure that had come, and the depth into which he had fallen, and "Peter went out and wept bitterly."

Oh! who can tell what that repentance must have been? During the following hours of that night, and the next day, when he saw Christ crucified and buried, and the next day, the Sabbath—oh, in what hopeless despair and shame he must have spent that day!

"My Lord is gone, my hope is gone, and I denied my Lord. After that life of love, after that blessed fellowship of three years, I denied my Lord. God have mercy upon me!"

I do not think we can realize into what a depth of humiliation Peter sank then. But that was the turning point and the change; and on the first day of the week Christ was seen of Peter, and in the evening He met him with the others. Later on at the Lake of Galilee He asked him: "Lovest thou me?" until Peter was made sad by the thought that the Lord reminded him of having denied Him thrice; and said in sorrow, but in uprightness: "Lord, thou knowest all things; thou knowest that I love thee."

Now Peter was prepared for *the deliverance from self*, and that is my last thought. You know Christ took him with others to the footstool of the throne, and bade them wait there; and then on the day of Pentecost the Holy Spirit came, and Peter was a changed man. I do not want you to think only of the change in Peter, in that boldness, and that power, and that insight into the Scriptures, and that blessing with which he preached that day. Thank God for that. But there was something for Peter deeper and better. Peter's whole nature was changed. The work that Christ began in Peter when He looked upon him, was perfected when he was filled with the Holy Ghost.

If you want to see that, read the First Epistle of Peter. You know wherein Peter's failings lay. When he said to Christ, in effect: "Thou never canst suffer; it cannot be"— it showed he had not a conception of what it was to pass through death into life. Christ said: "Deny thyself," and in spite of that he denied his Lord. When Christ warned him: "Thou shalt deny me," and he insisted that he never would, Peter showed how little he understood what there was in himself. But when I read his epistle and hear him say: "If ye be reproached for the name of Christ, happy are ye, for the Spirit of God and of glory resteth upon you," then I say that it is not the old Peter, but that is the very Spirit of Christ breathing and speaking within him.

I read again how he says: "Hereunto ye are called, to suffer, even as Christ suffered." I understand what a change had come over Peter. Instead of denying Christ, he found joy and pleasure in having self denied and crucified and given up to the death. And therefore it is in the *Acts* we read that, when he was called before the Council, he could boldly say: "We must obey God rather than men," and that he could return with the other disciples and rejoice that they were counted worthy to suffer for Christ's name.

You remember his self-exaltation; but now he has found out that "the ornament of a meek and quiet spirit is in the sight of God of great price." Again he tells us to be "subject one to another, and be clothed with humility."

Dear friend, I beseech you, look at Peter utterly changed—the self-pleasing, the self-trusting, the self-seeking Peter, full of sin, continually getting into trouble, foolish and impetuous, but now filled with the Spirit and the life of Jesus. Christ had done it for him by the Holy Ghost.

And now, what is my object in having thus very briefly pointed to the story of Peter? That story must be the history of every believer who is really to be made a blessing by God. That story is a prophecy of what everyone can receive from God in Heaven.

Now let us just glance hurriedly at what these lessons teach us.

The *first lesson* is this: You may be a very earnest, godly, devoted believer, in whom the power of the flesh is yet very strong.

That is a very solemn truth. Peter, before he denied Christ, had cast out devils and had healed the sick; and yet the flesh had power, and the flesh had room in him. Oh, beloved, we want to realize that it is just because there is so much of that self-life in us that the power of God cannot work in us as mightily as God is willing that it should work. Do you realize that the great God is longing to double His blessing, to give tenfold blessing through us? But there is something hindering Him, and that something is a proof of nothing but the self-life. We talk about the pride of Peter, and the impetuosity of Peter, and the self-confidence of Peter. It all rooted in that one word, *self*. Christ had said, "Deny self," and Peter had never understood, and never obeyed; and every failing came out of that.

What a solemn thought, and what an urgent plea for us to cry: O God, do discover this to us, that none of us may be living the self-life! It has happened to many a one who had been a Christian for years, who had perhaps occupied a prominent position, that God found him out and taught him to find himself out, and he became utterly ashamed, falling down broken before God. Oh, the bitter shame and sorrow and pain and agony that came to him, until at last he found that there was deliverance! Peter went out and wept bitterly, and there may be many a godly one in whom the power of the flesh still rules.

And then my *second lesson* is: It is the work of our blessed Lord Jesus to discover the power of self.

How was it that Peter, the carnal Peter, self-willed Peter, Peter with the strong self-love, ever became a man of Pentecost and the writer of his epistle? It was because Christ had him in charge, and Christ watched over him, and Christ taught and blessed him. The warnings that Christ had given him were part of the training; and last of all there came that look of love. In His suffering Christ did not forget him, but turned round and looked upon him, and "Peter went out and wept bitterly." And the Christ who led Peter to Pentecost is waiting today to take charge of every heart that is willing to surrender itself to Him.

Are there not some saying: "Ah! that is the mischief with me; it is always the self-life, and self-comfort, and self-consciousness, and self-pleasing, and self-will; how am I to get rid of it?"

My answer is: It is Christ Jesus who can rid you of it; none else but Christ Jesus can give deliverance from the power of self. And what does He ask you to do? He asks that you should humble yourself before Him.

7

Absolute Surrender

"And Ben-hadad the king of Syria gathered all his host together: and there were thirty and two kings with him, and horses, and chariots: and he went up and besieged Samaria, and warred against it. And he sent messengers to Ahab king of Israel into the city, and said unto him, Thus saith Ben-hadad Thy silver and thy gold is mine; thy wives also and thy children, even the goodliest, are mine. And the king of Israel answered and said, My lord, O king, according to thy saying, I am thine and all that I have." 1 Kings 20:1–4

W hat Ben-hadad asked was *absolute surrender;* and what Ahab gave was what was asked of him— *absolute surrender.* I want to use these words: "My lord, O king, according to thy saying, I am thine, and all that I have," as the words of absolute surrender with which every child of God ought to yield himself to his Father. We have heard it before, but we need to hear it very definitely—the condition of God's blessing is absolute surrender of all into His hands. Praise God! if our hearts are willing for that, there is no end to what God will do for us, and to the blessing God will bestow.

Absolute surrender—let me tell you where I got those

words. I used them myself often, and you have heard them numberless times. But in Scotland once I was in a company where we were talking about the condition of Christ's Church, and what the great need of the Church and of believers is; and there was in our company a godly worker who has much to do in training workers, and I asked him what he would say was the great need of the Church, and the message that ought to be preached. He answered very quietly and simply and determinedly: *"Absolute surrender to God is the one thing."* The words struck me as never before. And that man began to tell how, in the workers with whom he had to deal, he finds that if they are sound on that point, even though they be backward, they are willing to be taught and helped, and they always improve; whereas others who are not sound there very often go back and leave the work. The condition for obtaining God's full blessing is *absolute surrender* to Him.

And now, I desire by God's grace to give to you this message—that your God in heaven answers the prayers which you have offered for blessing on yourselves and for blessing on those around you by this one demand: *Are you willing to surrender yourselves absolutely into His hands?* What is our answer to be? God knows there are hundreds of hearts who have said it, and there are hundreds more who long to say it but hardly dare to do so. And there are hearts who have said it, but who have yet miserably failed, and who feel themselves condemned because they did not find the secret of the power to live that life. May God have a word for all!

Let me say, first of all, *God claims it from us.*

Yes, it has its foundation in the very nature of God. God cannot do otherwise. Who is God? He is the Fountain of life, the only Source of existence and power and goodness, and throughout the universe there is nothing good but what God works. God has created the sun, and the moon, and the stars, and the flowers, and the trees, and the grass; and are they not all absolutely surrendered to God? Do they not allow God to work in them just what He pleases? When God clothes the lily with its beauty, is it not yielded up, surrendered, given over to God as He works in it its beauty? And God's redeemed children, oh, can you think that God can work His work if there is only half or a part of them surrendered? God cannot do it. God is life, and love, and blessing, and power, and infinite beauty, and God delights to communicate Himself to every child who is prepared to receive Him; but ah! this one want of absolute surrender is just the thing that hinders God. And now He comes, and as God He claims it.

You know in daily life what absolute surrender is. You know that everything has to be given up to its special, definite object and service. I have a pen in my pocket, and that pen is absolutely surrendered to the one work of writing, and that pen must be absolutely surrendered to my hand if I am to write properly with it. If another holds it partly, I cannot write properly. This coat is absolutely given up to me to cover my body. This building is entirely given up to religious services. And now, do you expect that in your immortal being, in the divine nature that you have received by regeneration, God can work His work, every day and every hour, unless you are entirely given up to Him? God cannot. The temple of Solomon was absolutely surrendered to God when it was dedicated to Him. And every one of us is a temple of God, in which God will dwell and work mightily on one condition— absolute surrender to Him. God claims it, God is worthy of it, and without it God cannot work His blessed work in us.

But secondly, God not only claims it, *but God will work it Himself.* I am sure there is many a heart that says: "Ah, but that absolute surrender implies so much!" Someone says: "Oh, I have passed through so much trial and suffering, and there is so much of the self-life still remaining, and I dare not face the entire giving of it up, because I know it will cause so much trouble and agony."

Alas! alas! that God's children have such thoughts of Him, such cruel thoughts. Oh, I come to you with a message, fearful and anxious one. God does not ask you to give the perfect surrender in your strength, or by the power of your will; God is willing to work it in you. Do we not read: "It is God that worketh in us, both to will and to do of His good pleasure"? And that is what we should seek for—to go on our faces before God, until our hearts learn to believe that the everlasting God Himself will come in to turn out what is wrong, to conquer what is evil, and to work what is well-pleasing in His blessed sight. God Himself will work it in you.

Look at the men in the Old Testament, like Abraham. Do you think it was by accident that God found that man, the father of the faithful and the friend of God, and that it was Abraham himself, apart from God, who had such faith and such obedience and such devotion? You know it is not so. God raised him up and prepared him as an instrument for His glory.

Did not God say to Pharaoh: "For this cause have I raised thee up, for to show in thee my power"? And if God said that of him, will not God say it *far more of every child of His?*

Oh, I want to encourage you, and I want you to cast away every fear. Come with that feeble desire; and if there is the fear which says: "Oh, my desire is not strong enough, I am not willing for everything that may come, I do not feel bold enough to say I can conquer everything"—I pray you, learn to know and trust your God now. Say: "My God, I am willing that Thou shouldst make me willing." If there is anything holding you back, or any sacrifice you are afraid of making, come to God now, and prove how gracious your God is, and be not afraid that He will command from you what He will not bestow.

God comes and offers to work this absolute surrender in you. All these searchings and hungerings and longings that are in your heart, I tell you they are the drawings of the divine magnet, Christ Jesus. He lived a life of absolute surrender, He has got possession of you, He is living in your heart by His Holy Spirit. You have hindered and hindered Him terribly, but He desires to help you to get hold of Him entirely. And He comes and draws you now by His message and words. Will you not come and trust God to work in you that absolute surrender to Himself? Yes, blessed be God, He can do it and He will do it.

The *third* thought. God not only claims it and works it, but *God accepts it when we bring it to Him.* God works it in the secret of our heart, God urges us by the hidden power of His Holy Spirit to come and speak it out, and we have to bring and to yield to Him that absolute surrender. But remember, when you come and bring God that absolute surrender, it may, as far as your feelings or your consciousness go, be a thing of great imperfection, and you may doubt and hesitate and say: "Is it absolute?"

But, oh, remember there was once a man to whom Christ had said: "If thou canst believe, all things are possible to him that believeth." And his heart was afraid, and he cried out: "Lord, I believe, help Thou mine unbelief."

That was a faith that triumphed over the devil, and the evil spirit was cast out. And if you come and say: "Lord, I yield myself in absolute surrender to my God," even though it be with a trembling heart and with the consciousness: "I do not feel the power, I do not feel the determination, I do not feel the assurance," it will succeed. Be not afraid, but come just as you are, and even in the midst of your trembling the power of the Holy Ghost will work.

Have you never yet learned the lesson that the Holy Ghost works with mighty power while on the human side everything appears feeble? Look at the Lord Jesus Christ in Gethsemane. We read that He, "through the Eternal Spirit," offered Himself a sacrifice unto God. The Almighty Spirit of God was enabling Him to do it. And yet what agony and fear and exceeding sorrow came over Him, and how He prayed! Externally you can see no sign of the mighty power of the Spirit, but the Spirit of God was there. And even so, while you are feeble and fighting and trembling, in faith in the hidden work of God's Spirit, do not fear, but yield yourself.

And when you do yield yourself in absolute surrender, let it be in the faith that God does now accept of it. That is the great point, and that is what we so often miss:—that believers should be thus occupied with God in this matter of surrender. I pray you, be occupied with God. We want to get help, every one of us, so that in our daily life God shall be clearer to us, God shall have the right place, and be "all in all." And if we are to have that through life, let us begin now and look away from ourselves, and look up to God. Let each believe,—while I, a poor worm on earth and a trembling child of God, full of failure and sin and fear, bow here, and no one knows what passes through my heart, and while I in simplicity say, O God, I accept Thy terms; I have pleaded for blessing on myself and others, I have accepted Thy terms of absolute surrender—while your heart says that in deep silence, remember there is a God present that takes note of it, and writes it down in His book, and there is a God present who at that very moment takes possession of you. You may not feel it, you may not realize it, but God takes possession if you will trust Him.

A *fourth* thought. God not only claims it, and works it, and accepts it when I bring it, *but God maintains it*. That is the great difficulty with many. People say: "I have often been stirred at a meeting, or at a convention, and I have consecrated myself to God, but it has passed away. I know it may last for a week or for a month, but away it fades, and after a time it is all gone."

But listen! It is because you do not believe what I am now going to tell you and remind you of. When God has begun the work of absolute surrender in you, and when God has accepted your surrender, then God holds Himself bound to care for it and to keep it. Will you believe that?

In this matter of surrender there are two, *God and I*

—I a worm, God the everlasting and omnipotent Jehovah.
Worm, will you be afraid to trust yourself to this mighty
God now? God is willing. Do you not believe that He
can keep you continually, day by day, and moment by
moment?

> Moment by moment I'm *kept* in His love;
> Moment by moment I've life from above.

If God allows the sun to shine upon you moment by
moment, without intermission, will not God let His life
shine upon you every moment? And why have you not
experienced it? Because you have not trusted God for it,
and you do not surrender yourself absolutely to God in
that trust.

A life of absolute surrender has its difficulties. I do not
deny that. Yea, it has something far more than difficulties;
it is a life that with men is absolutely impossible. But by
the grace of God, by the power of God, by the power of
the Holy Spirit dwelling in us, it is a life to which we are
destined, and a life that is possible for us, praise God! Let
us believe that God will maintain it.

Some of you read recently the words of that aged
saint who, on his ninetieth birthday, told of all God's
goodness to him—I mean George Muller. What did he
say he believed to be the secret of his happiness, and of
all the blessing with which God had visited him? He said
he believed there were two reasons. The one was that he
had been enabled by grace to maintain a good conscience
before God day by day; the other was, that he was a lover
of God's Word. Ah, yes, a good conscience in unfeigned

obedience to God day by day, and fellowship with God every day in His Word, and prayer—that is a life of absolute surrender.

Such a life has two sides—on the one side, *absolute surrender to work what God wants you to do;* on the other side, *to let God work what He wants to do.*

First, *to do what God wants you to do.* Give up yourselves absolutely to the will of God. You know something of that will; not enough, far from all. But say absolutely to the Lord God: "By Thy grace I desire to do Thy will in everything, every moment of every day." Say: "Lord God, not a word upon my tongue but for Thy glory, not a movement of my temper but for Thy glory, not an affection of love or hate in my heart but for Thy glory, and according to Thy blessed will."

Someone says: "Do you think that possible?"

I ask, What has God promised you, and what can God do to fill a vessel absolutely surrendered to Him? Oh, God wants to bless you in a way beyond what you expect. From the beginning ear hath not heard, neither hath the eye seen, what God hath prepared for them that wait for Him. God has prepared unheard-of things you never can think of; blessings much more wonderful than you can imagine, more mighty than you can conceive. They are divine blessings. Oh, say now: "I give myself absolutely to God, to His will, to do only what God wants." It is God who will enable you to carry out the surrender.

And, on the other side, come and say: "I give myself absolutely to God, *to let Him work in me to will and to do of His good pleasure,* as He has promised to do."

Yes, the living God wants to work in His children in

a way that we cannot understand, but that God's Word has revealed, and He wants to work in us every moment of the day. God is willing to maintain our life. Only let our absolute surrender be one of simple, childlike, and unbounded trust.

The last thought. This absolute surrender to God *will wonderfully bless us.* What Ahab said to his enemy, King Ben-hadad,—"My lord, O king, according to thy word I am thine, and all that I have"—shall we not say to our God and loving Father? If we do say it, God's blessing will come upon us. God wants us to be separate from the world; we are called to come out from the world that hates God. Come out for God, and say: "Lord, anything for Thee." If you say that with prayer, and speak that into God's ear, He will accept it, and He will teach you what it means.

I say again, God will bless you. You have been praying for blessing. But do remember, there must be absolute surrender. At every tea-table you see it. Why is tea poured into that cup? Because it is empty, and given up for the tea. But put ink, or vinegar, or wine into it, and will they pour the tea into the vessel? And can God fill you, can God bless you if you are not absolutely surrendered to Him? He cannot. Let us believe God has wonderful blessings for us, if we will but stand up for God, and say, be it with a trembling will, yet with a believing heart: "O God, I accept Thy demands. I am thine and all that I have. Absolute surrender is what my soul yields to Thee by divine grace."

You may not have such strong and clear feelings of deliverance as you would desire to have, but humble yourselves in His sight, and acknowledge that you have grieved the Holy Spirit by your self-will, self-confidence, and self-effort. Bow humbly before Him in the confession of that, and ask him to break the heart and to bring you into the dust before Him. Then, as you bow before Him, just accept God's teaching that in your flesh "there dwelleth no good thing," and that nothing will help you except another life which must come in. You must deny self once for all. Denying self must every moment be the power of your life, and then Christ will come in and take possession of you.

When was Peter delivered? When was the change accomplished? The change began with Peter weeping, and the Holy Ghost came down and filled his heart.

God the Father loves to give us the power of the Spirit. We have the Spirit of God dwelling within us. We come to God confessing that, and praising God for it; and yet confessing how we have grieved the Spirit. And then we bow our knees to the Father to ask that He would strengthen us with all might by the Spirit in the inner man, and that He would fill us with His mighty power. And as the Spirit reveals Christ to us, Christ comes to live in our hearts forever, and the self-life is cast out.

Let us bow before God in humiliation, and in that humiliation confess before Him the state of the whole Church. No words can tell the sad state of the Church of Christ on earth. I wish I had words to speak what I sometimes feel about it. Just think of the Christians around you. I do not speak of nominal Christians, or of professing Christians, but I speak of hundreds and thousands of honest, earnest Christians who are not living a life in the power of

God or to His glory. So little power, so little devotion or consecration to God, so little conception of the truth that a Christian is a man utterly surrendered to God's will! Oh, we want to confess the sins of God's people around us, and to humble ourselves. We are members of that sickly body, and the sickliness of the body will hinder us, and break us down, unless we come to God, and in confession separate ourselves from partnership with worldliness, with coldness towards each other, unless we give up ourselves to be entirely and wholly for God.

How much Christian work is being done in the spirit of the flesh, and in the power of self! How much work, day by day, in which human energy—our will and our thoughts about the work—is continually manifested, and in which there is but little of waiting upon God, and upon the power of the Holy Ghost! Let us make confession. But as we confess the state of the Church and the feebleness and sinfulness of work for God among us, let us come back to ourselves. Who is there who truly longs to be delivered from the power of the self-life, who truly acknowledges that it *is* the power of self and the flesh, and who is willing to cast all at the feet of Christ? *There is deliverance.*

I heard of one who had been an earnest Christian, and who spoke about the "cruel" thought of separation and death. But you do not think that, do you? What are we to think of separation and death? This:—Death was the path to glory for Christ. For the joy set before Him He endured the cross. The cross was the birthplace of His everlasting glory. Do you love Christ? Do you long to be *in* Christ, and not *like* Him? Let death be to you the most desirable thing on earth; death to self, and fellowship with Christ.

Separation—do you think it a hard thing to be called to be entirely free from the world, and by that separation to be united to God and His love, by separation to become prepared for living and walking with God every day? Surely one ought to say:

"Anything to bring me to separation, to death, for a life of full fellowship with God and Christ."

Oh! come and cast this self-life and flesh-life at the feet of Jesus. Then trust Him. Do not worry yourselves with trying to understand all about it, but come in the living faith that Christ will come into you with the power of His death and the power of His life; and then the Holy Spirit will bring the whole Christ—Christ crucified and Christ risen and living in glory—into your heart.

8

Christ Our Life

"Christ who is our life." Colossians 3:4

I am certain that many who joined in our act of surrender last night have felt, as I have felt: O God, how little we understand it! And that they have prayed: Lord, God, Thou must Thyself take possession, if we are to know what it really means. But we believe, as we said, that through faith on our part He does accept, although the experience and the power of that absolute surrender do not come at once, and that it is ours to hold fast our attitude before God until the experience and power do come.

But let me now add, what was only mentioned in passing last night that *if this absolute surrender is to be maintained and lived out, it must be by having Christ coming into our life in new power.* That is the thought of which I wish to speak this morning. It is only in Christ that we can draw nigh to God, and it is only in Christ that God can draw nigh to us. We need to have "Christ our life." Beloved, we are here pleading with God to work mightily in London and in the world, in the power of the Holy Ghost, for the sanctification of His people and for the conversion of sinners. What we need is that *what we ask God to do in others should be fully done in ourselves.*

We want to let God reveal Christ to take entire possession of us, and then Christ will be able to work through us above what we ask or think.

The thoughts I want to put before you in illustration of this great truth, "Christ our life," are four very simple ones. If we want to understand those words, let us consider, first, *Christ before us as our Example*; secondly, *Christ for us as our Propitiation*; thirdly, *Christ with us as our Saviour from sin*; and lastly, *Christ in us as our strength and our life*. O Lord, while man has to speak, give Thy grace, that we may not cover ourselves with any covering but the covering of Thy Spirit. Lord God, awaken in the heart of speaker and hearers the realization that we are all children of Thy family, bowing before Thy feet. Awaken in every heart a deep faith that our God, by the Holy Spirit, is going to reveal Christ to us even now. Our Father, we wait on Thee. Our soul doth wait, and our hope is in Thy word.

If Christ is to be our life we must look, in the first place, as:

1. *Christ before us as our example*. When I speak of Christ as my life, it must not be a vague indefinite thing, but I must *know*. Life always works itself out in conduct and action, and I want to realize that if Christ comes into me as my life, it must not only be something hidden in my heart, but something that proves itself in every action and in every moment of my existence. And if I want to know how it will show itself, what my sentiments and words and actions and habits will be if I have Christ's life, I must go to the life of the Lord Jesus upon earth and study that. And as I study the life and walk of God's own beloved Son, I

must remember that before God took Him up to heaven, God let Him live here upon earth, that in His life I might have a picture, a revelation, a complete representation of what my God wanted me to be, and was willing to make me. That is the light in which you must study the life of Christ in the Gospels not the only, but one most important, light.

And what do I find, then, as I look at Christ? We spoke last night of absolute surrender to God. That was the very root of Christ's life. He came as a man whom God had sent into the world, and as a man who had nothing to do but to fulfil the will of God; and He came as a man who had nothing in Himself, but who everyday depended upon God and waited for God to teach Him, and to speak words through Him, and to show Him the works He had to do. "The Son can do nothing of Himself." He lived a life of absolute surrender to God. God's will, God's honour, God's kingdom. He lived and He died for them, and He did it, not under strain at certain times, throwing it off at other times to seek relaxation in something of the world, and forgetting to hold communication with God, as many Christians do. Religion to them is a strain and a burden and a duty, and it is so delightful just to relax a little and throw off the strain. Ah, no! God was Christ's joy, and the Fountain of living waters to Him, and it was His delight and His strength to live in God and for God. The will of God was His meat and refreshment and strength.

And God comes to all of us who ask this morning: My God, I gave the vow last night of absolute surrender, and thou knowest that, though it was done in feebleness and in trembling, it was done in honesty and in uprightness;

but my God, what does it mean? How am I to live that life? The Father points to the beloved Son, and He says, "This is My beloved Son, in whom I am well pleased. Hear Him, follow Him, live like Him, let Christ be the law of your life."

Let us yield our hearts to God in prayer, for Him to search us and discover to us whether the life of Christ has actually been the law that we have taken for the guide of our life. I do not speak about attainment, but let us ask, Have I actually said: Oh, how blessed it would be! Oh, this is what I covet, and what I wait upon God for! I want to live for God in the way Christ lived? It almost sounds as if it were too high and presumptuous. But what does Christ mean when He said so often: As I, even so you; as I loved, even so love one another; as I kept the commandments of My Father, so if ye keep His commandments, ye shall abide in My Love? What does the Holy Spirit mean when He says, "Let this mind be in you which was also in Christ Jesus, who made Himself of no reputation, but humbled Himself and became obedient unto death"? The mind of Christ must be my mind, my disposition, and my life.

There is many a man who wants eternal life in heaven from Christ, but who does not want the life here on earth which Christ lived. And there is many a believer who has written it down, alas,—"There can be no thought of imitating and following Christ with any measure of exactness"; he does not aim to come near to Christ. But if last night you honestly said: Father, Thou hast a right to it, and my heart gives absolute surrender to God from henceforth; then come this morning and say: The life of Christ must become mine.

But secondly. If we want to know what this means, "Christ our life," we must not only look at Christ and His work before us as our example.

2. *Christ for us as our Propitiation.* In His life Christ prepared the path in which we are to walk. He left us an example that we should follow in His footsteps; He marked out the road in which we were to move on the way to eternal life. But that was not enough, for we were shut out from that path and that life, by sin and its curse, death. And so Christ, after having prepared and marked out the blessed path, went Himself down into the suffering and the death of Calvary, giving up His will to God unto the death. There He bore our sins and our curse, and the chastisement of our peace was laid upon Him, that by His stripes we might be healed. He gave His precious blood, "the blood of the everlasting covenant," that by it He might gain an entrance for us into the very presence of our God.

And now Christ is there as our High Priest, to apply within our hearts, as a living Saviour, the divine power of that propitiation. And whenever we think of drawing nigh to God, and of serving God and of offering ourselves unto God, and the thought comes up and it is right that we should thus look at it—I in my sinfulness, I with my transgressions and backslidings since I was converted and received Christ, I with the sinfulness of my nature, can I actually have fellowship with God every day? Then the answer comes: We have been made nigh by the blood of Jesus. "Having... boldness by the blood of Jesus, let us draw near."

Were there any of you last night who felt afraid to make

the great surrender, the absolute surrender, because you felt too unworthy? Oh, think of this; your worthiness is not in yourself, or in the intensity or uprightness of your consecration; your worthiness is in Christ Jesus. We read in God's Word, it is "the altar that sanctifieth the gift," and we know that Christ is not only the Priest and the Victim, "the Lamb that was slain," but that the living Christ is Himself the Altar. Seven days the altar was to be sanctified by a sevenfold blood sprinkling; and after that God said, That altar shall be an altar most holy: whatsoever toucheth the altar shall be holy. And in the New Testament we are taught that "the altar sanctifieth the gift." Christ is our Altar. Oh, if there is anyone afraid, and asking, can God accept me in my feebleness? Come, child of God, and be not afraid. Lay yourself upon Christ, the living Altar, the everlasting Propitiation, who can make you acceptable to God every moment; and rest there. Rest upon Him in the sweet consciousness and faith. All unworthy and all feeble though I be, the altar sanctifieth the gift, and in Jesus and resting on Him, my God accepts my feebleness, and I am well pleasing in His sight. Oh, Christians, seek to maintain it as the power of continual access to God. "If we walk in the light, the blood of Jesus Christ His Son cleanseth us from all sin." It is in Christ that the door to the heart of my Father is open every moment; it is in the blood of the blessed Lamb of God that every moment from above, the inflowing of the divine life can come into your heart and mine.

But thirdly, I have not only Christ before me as my Example, and Christ for me as my Propitiation, but I have...

3. *Christ with me as my Saviour from sin, my Friend, my Leader, and my Guide.* Yes, that was the precious promise of our gracious Lord ere He left. "Lo I am with you always." And earlier than that He had said, when the disciples could not yet understand Him, "Where two or three are gathered together in My name, there I am in the midst of them."

What you and I need to realise is this: that Jesus Christ is nearer to us than our nearest earthly friend. Ah! if we would but take time to turn our eyes and hearts away from this world, and from all the loving faces and friends that surround us, and all the joys that attract us, and all the love that greets us, and fix them steadfastly and humbly and trustingly on the face and the love and the joy of Jesus, He is able so to manifest Himself to us that our hearts shall be filled with the consciousness—Jesus is with me. You know how deep in the consciousness of a father, for instance, every morning as he rises, is the thought: I have beloved children, I have a beloved wife, I have a family; we meet at breakfast. It is so natural, the whole heart is full of it, it does not need a moment's thought. Can it be that Christ can make His presence as near and as clear and as dear to me as the fellowship of the dearest ones upon earth? *Christ can do it*, and Christ *longs* to do it, and Christ is worthy that we should let Him do it.

O God, when will the time come when Thy Son will be to us nearer than father or mother, wife or husband, child or brother? Oh, hasten that blessed hour!

Jesus Christ wants to live with you, and to walk with you, that He may do this blessed work for you. He wants to be with you as your Companion, so that you never shall be alone. No trial, no difficulty, no fire, no water through which you have to pass, but in which the promise of Jehovah, in the Old Testament, "I will be with thee," will not be fulfilled to you in Christ Jesus. No battle that you have to fight with sin or temptation, no feebleness that makes you tremble in the consciousness of what you are yourself, but it is possible to have Christ as Leader, to show you the way in which you have to walk; Jesus Christ as Companion, to comfort you by His presence, and make your heart glad; Jesus Christ as Saviour from sin, in His mighty power watching over you, and working in you all God's good pleasure. Oh that God might show us that the life of absolute surrender is a life that can be lived in Christ Jesus, a life that can be lived because Christ Himself will care for us and watch over us.

And then comes the last thought:

4. *Christ in us as our life and our strength.* That is the crown of all. The young convert ordinarily understands very little of that. Many a believer has lived long in some experience of Christ with Him as Guide and Helper, but has never yet come to realise what this other means: Christ in me, my very life and my very strength. And yet that is what the Apostle Paul tells us is the great gospel mystery, the mystery that was hid for ages and generations, but has now been revealed; the mystery of God's people, of which he says "the riches of the glory of this mystery, which is Christ in you." Christians, the riches and glory of our God in heaven are manifest to you in this: God wants you to have Christ His Son living in you. Oh, may we come to that today not to ask for a little blessing, a beginning of blessings, but to have our whole life opened up to the

indwelling, to the control, to the sanctifying power of Jesus Christ.

We speak to workers. Our great thought has been that of *work*. What is needed if God is to bless all these workers who have gathered together here? How is God's power to come and to work? Beloved, Christ is the power of God, and we want more of Christ, we want the whole Christ, we want Christ in every one of us revealed by the Holy Ghost, and then the power of God will work.

Yesterday morning we spoke of a church so filled with the Holy Ghost, that the Holy Ghost could say to that church: Set apart for Me the men that I have called for My work. And we spoke of workers as people who are fit and ready and willing to be set apart for the Holy Ghost. How can each church be brought to this condition? In one way only. John the Baptist preached Christ who baptized "with the Holy Ghost and with fire." That tells me Jesus Christ is the One from whom the Holy Ghost must flow into us in ever new and larger measure; and if you want the power of God's Spirit to be revealed where you are, or away in heathendom, it must come from a closer attachment to Christ; a closer union with Him, a larger revelation of Christ dwelling in Christian people. A blessing then must come. Did not Jesus say, "He that believeth on Me, out of him shall flow rivers of living water"? And is not this by faith, *by believing, that Christ comes and dwells in the heart*, and becomes Himself the Fountain out of which the Holy Spirit flows? What do we read in the last chapter of the Revelation of St. John? "And He showed me a pure river of water of life, clear as crystal, proceeding out of the throne of God and of the Lamb." Yes, the Lamb went and sat down upon the throne of glory, and the river of water of life flowed out. It is the Lamb who must lead you and me to the fountains of living water, and give them within our hearts, so that we shall have power to work among men—not the power of reason, not the power of human love, and zeal, and earnestness, and diligence, but the power that comes from God.

Are you ready for that power? Are you ready to surrender yourself absolutely to God and receive it? Can you truly say: Lord, I am utterly given up to Thee. It is done feebly, tremblingly, but, Lord God, it is done. I have received but little of what I know my God can give, but as an empty vessel, cleansed and lowly, I place myself at Thy feet again, day by day, and moment by moment, and I wait upon my God? And, child of God, what eye hath not seen nor ear heard, and what men have never been able to conceive, what you have not conceived, God will do for them that wait for Him, and for them that love Him.

Our Convention will profit us very little unless it lead us closer up to God, and to have larger expectations from God, and closer fellowship with God. How can that be? Christ Jesus can do it for us. Christ is our life. He will live in us the same life He lived upon earth. Shall we not expect Him to do it in the fullness of His promise? Shall we not come with every sin and every hindrance and every shortcoming and everything that causes self condemnation, and cast it all at His feet, and believe the blood cleanses, and Jesus gives deliverance? Do believe, and then expect it and accept it, that God Himself will reveal Christ within us in the power of the Holy Spirit. God grant it to every beloved worker gathered here.

9

"We Can Love all the day."

"The fruit of the spirit is love." Galatians 5:22

I want to look at the fact of a life filled with the Holy Spirit more from the practical side, and to show how this life will show itself in our daily walk and conduct.

Under the Old Testament you know the Holy Spirit often came upon men as a Divine Spirit of revelation, to reveal the mysteries of God, or for power to do the work of God. But He did not then dwell in them. Now, many just want the Old Testament gift of power for work, but know very little of the New Testament gift of the indwelling Spirit, animating and renewing the whole life. When God gives the Holy Spirit, His great object is the formation of a holy character. It is a gift of a holy mind and spiritual disposition, and what we need above everything else, is to say:

"I must have the Holy Spirit sanctifying my whole inner life if I am really to live for God's glory."

You might say that when Christ promised the Spirit to the disciples He did so that they might have power to be witnesses. True, but then they received the Holy Ghost in such heavenly power and reality that He took possession of their whole being at once and so fitted them as holy men for doing the work with power as they had to do it. Christ spoke of power to the disciples, but it was the Spirit filling their whole being that worked the power.

I wish now to dwell upon the passage found in Gal. 5: 22: "The fruit of the Spirit is love."

We read that "Love is the fulfilling of the law," and my desire is to speak on love as a fruit of the Spirit with a twofold object. One is that this word may be a searchlight in our hearts, and give us a test by which to try all our thoughts about the Holy Spirit and all our experience of the holy life. Let us try ourselves by this word. Has this been our daily habit, to seek the being filled with the Holy Spirit as the Spirit of love? "The fruit of the Spirit is love." Has it been our experience that the more we have of the Holy Spirit the more loving we become? In claiming the Holy Spirit we should make this the first object of our expectation. The Holy Spirit comes as a Spirit of love.

Oh, if this were true in the Church of Christ how different her state would be! May God help us to get hold of this simple heavenly truth, that the fruit of the Spirit is a love which appears in the life, and that just as the Holy Spirit gets real possession of the life, the heart will be filled with real, divine, universal love.

You can easily understand why I chose this subject for this afternoon. On Tuesday evening we spoke about the different objects that we had in this gathering, and one was to bring together and to unite closer all the workers in East London, and if possible in London and elsewhere, in one spirit and one body. We said, and you all believe, that one of the great causes why God cannot bless is *the want of love*. When the body is divided, there cannot be strength.

I am going to Holland, if God will, tomorrow evening. In the time of their great religious wars, when Holland stood out so nobly against Spain, one of their mottoes was: "Unity gives strength." And you know how it is only when God's people stand as one body, one before God in the fellowship of love, one towards another in deep affection, one before the world in a love that the world can see—it is only then that they will have power to secure the blessing which they ask of God. Remember that if a vessel that ought to be one whole is cracked into many pieces, it cannot be filled. You can take a potsherd, one part of a vessel, and dip out a little water into that, but if you want the vessel full, the vessel must be whole. That is literally true of Christ's Church, and if there is one thing we must pray for still, it is this: Lord melt us together into one by the power of the Holy Spirit; let the Holy Spirit, who at Pentecost made them all of one heart and one soul, do His blessed work among us. Praise God, we can love each other in a divine love, for "the fruit of the Spirit is love." Give yourselves up to love, and the Holy Spirit will come; receive the Spirit, and He will teach you to love more.

Now, why is it that the fruit of the Spirit is love? *Because God is love*. And what does that mean?

It is the very nature and being of God to delight in communicating Himself. God has no selfishness, God keeps nothing to Himself. God's nature is to be always giving. In the sun and the moon and the stars, in every flower you see it, in every bird in the air, in every fish in the sea. God communicates life to His creatures. And the angels around His throne, the seraphim and cherubim who are flames of fire—whence have they their glory? It is because God is love, and He imparts to them of His brightness and His blessedness. And we, His redeemed children—God delights to pour His love into us. And why? Because, as I said, God keeps nothing for Himself. From eternity God had His only begotten Son, and the Father gave Him all things, and nothing that God had was kept back. "God is love."

One of the old Church fathers said that we cannot better understand the Trinity than as a revelation of divine love—the Father the loving One, the Fountain of love; the Son the beloved one, the Reservoir of love, in whom the love was poured out; and the Spirit the living love that united both and then overflowed into this world. The Spirit of Pentecost, the Spirit of the Father, and the Spirit of the Son is love. And when the Holy Spirit comes to us and to other men, will He be less a Spirit of love than He is in God? It cannot be; He cannot change His nature. The Spirit of God is love, and "the fruit of the Spirit is love."

Why is that so? That was the one great need of mankind, that was the thing which Christ's redemption came to accomplish: *to restore love to this world.* When man sinned, why was it that he sinned? Selfishness triumphed—he sought self instead of God. And just look! Adam at once begins to accuse the woman of having led him astray. Love to God had gone, love to man was lost. Look again: of the first two children of Adam, the one becomes a murderer of his brother. Does not that teach us that sin had robbed the world of love? Ah! what a proof the history of the world has been of love having been lost!

There may have been beautiful examples of love even among the heathen, but only as a little remnant of what was lost. One of the worst things sin did for man was to make him selfish, for selfishness cannot love. The Lord Jesus Christ came down from heaven as the Son of God's love. "God so loved the world that He gave His only begotten Son." God's Son came to show what love is, and He lived a life of love here upon earth in fellowship with His disciples, in compassion over the poor and miserable, in love even to His enemies, and He died the death of love. And when He went to heaven, whom did He send down? The Spirit of love, to come and banish selfishness and envy and pride, and bring the love of God into the hearts of men. "The fruit of the Spirit is love."

And what was the preparation for the promise of the Holy Spirit? You know that promise as found in the fourteenth chapter of John's gospel. But remember what precedes in the thirteenth chapter. Before Christ promised the Holy Spirit He gave a new commandment, and about that new commandment He said wonderful things. One thing was: "Even as I have loved you, so love ye one another." To them His dying love was to be the only law of their conduct and intercourse with each other. What a message to those fishermen, to those men full of pride and selfishness! "Learn to love each other," said Christ, "as I have loved you." And by the grace of God they did it. When Pentecost came they were of one heart and one soul. Christ did it for them. And now He calls us to dwell and to walk in love. He demands that though a man hate you, still you love him. True love cannot be conquered by anything in heaven or upon the earth. The more hatred there is, the more love triumphs through it all and shows its true nature. This is the love that Christ commanded His disciples to exercise,

What more did He say? "By this shall all men know that ye are my disciples, if ye have love one to another." You all know what it is to wear a badge. Many of you wear a blue ribbon badge, and everybody knows what that means. And Christ said to His disciples in effect: "I give you a badge, and that badge is *Love*. That is to be your mark. It is the only thing in heaven or on earth by which men can know me." Oh! do not we begin to fear that *love has fled from the earth?* That if we were to ask the world: "Have you seen us wear the badge of love?" the world would say: "No; what we have heard of the Church of Christ is that there is not a place where there is no quarrelling and separation." Let us ask God with one heart that we may wear the badge of Jesus' love. God is able to give it.

"The fruit of the Spirit is love." Why? *Because nothing but love can expel and conquer our selfishness.* Self is the great curse, whether in its relation to God, or to our fellow men in general, or to fellow Christians; thinking of ourselves and seeking our own. Self is our greatest curse. But, praise God, Christ came to redeem us from self. We sometimes talk about deliverance from the self-life—and thank God for every word that can be said about it to help us—but I am afraid some people think deliverance from the self-life means that now they are going to have no longer any trouble in serving God; and they forget that *deliverance from self-life means to be a vessel overflowing with love to everybody all the day.*

And there you have the reason why many people pray for the power of the Holy Ghost, and they get something, but oh, so little! because they prayed for power for work, and power for blessing, but they have not prayed for power for full deliverance from self. That means not only the righteous self in intercourse with God, but the unloving self in intercourse with men. And there *is* deliverance. "The fruit of the Spirit is love." I bring you the glorious promise of Christ that He is able to fill our hearts with love.

A great many of us try hard at times to love. We try to force ourselves to love, and I do not say that is wrong; it is better than nothing. But the end of it is always very sad. "I fail continually," such an one must confess. And what is the reason? The reason is simply this: Because they have never learned to believe and accept the truth that the Holy Spirit can pour God's love into their heart. That blessed text; often it has been limited!—"The love of God is shed abroad in our hearts." It has often been understood in this sense: It means the love of God *to me.* Oh, what a limitation! That is only the beginning. The love of God is always the love of God in its entirety, in its fullness as an indwelling power, a love of God to me that leaps back to Him in love, and overflows to my fellow men in love—God's love to me, and my love to God, and my love to my fellow men. The three are one; you cannot separate them. Do believe that the love of God can be shed abroad in your heart and mine so that we can love all the day.

"Ah!" you say, "how little I have understood that!"

Why is a lamb always gentle? Because that is its nature. Does it cost the lamb any trouble to be gentle? No. Why not? It *is* so beautiful and gentle. Has a lamb to study to be gentle? No. Why does that come so easy? It is its nature. And a wolf—why does it cost a wolf no trouble to be cruel, and to put its fangs into the poor lamb or sheep? Because that is its nature. It has not to summon up its courage; the wolf-nature is there.

And how can I learn to love? Never until the Spirit of God fills my heart with God's love, and I begin to long for God's love in a very different sense from which I have sought it so selfishly, as a comfort and a joy and a happiness and a pleasure to myself; never until I begin to learn that "God is love," and to claim it, and receive it as an indwelling power for self-sacrifice; never until I begin to see that my glory, my blessedness, is to be like God and like Christ, in giving up everything in myself for my fellow-men. May God teach us that! Oh, the divine blessedness of the love with which the Holy Spirit can fill our hearts! "The fruit of the Spirit is love."

Once again I ask, Why must this be so? And my answer is: *Without this we cannot live the daily life of love.* How often, when we speak about the consecrated life, we have to speak about *temper,* and some people have sometimes said: "You make too much of temper." I do not think we can make too much of it. Do you see yonder clock? You know what those hands mean. The hands tell me what is within the clock, and if I see that the hands stand still, and that the hands point wrong, and that the clock is slow or fast, I say that there is something inside the clock that is wrong. And temper is just like the revelation that the clock gives of what is within. Temper is a proof whether the love of Christ is filling the heart, or not. How many there are who find it easier in church, or in the prayer-meeting, or in work for the Lord, diligent, earnest work, to be holy and happy than in the daily life with wife and children and servant; easier to be holy and happy outside the home than in it. Where is the love of God? In Christ. God has prepared for us a wonderful redemption in Christ, and He longs to make something supernatural of us. Have we learned to long for it, and ask for it, and expect it in its fullness?

Then there is the *tongue!* We sometimes speak of the tongue when we talk of the better life and the restful life, but just think what liberty many Christians give to their tongues. They say: "I have a right to think what I like." When they speak about each other, when they speak about their neighbours, when they speak about other Christians, how often there are sharp remarks! God keep me from saying anything that would be unloving; God shut my mouth if I am not to speak in tender love. But what I am saying is a fact. How often there is found among Christians who are banded together in work, sharp criticism, sharp judgment, hasty opinion, unloving words, secret contempt of each other, secret condemnation of each other. Oh, just as a mother's love covers her children and delights in them and has the tenderest compassion with their foibles or failures, so there ought to be in the heart of every believer a motherly love toward every brother and sister in Christ. Have you aimed at that? Have you sought it? Have you ever pleaded for it? Jesus Christ said: "As I have loved you... love one another." And He did not put that among the other commandments, but He said in effect: "That is a New commandment, the one commandment: Love one another as I have loved you."

It is in our daily life and conduct that the fruit of the Spirit is love. From that there comes all the graces and virtues in which love is manifested: joy, peace, longsuffering, gentleness, goodness; no sharpness or hardness in your tone, no unkindness or selfishness; meekness before God and man. You see that all these are the gentler virtues. I have often thought as I read those words in Colossians, "Put on therefore as the elect of God, holy and beloved, bowels of mercies, kindness, humbleness of mind, meekness, longsuffering," that if we had written, we should have put in the foreground the manly virtues, such as zeal, courage and diligence; but we need to see how the gentler, the most womanly virtues are specially connected with dependence upon the Holy Spirit. These are indeed heavenly graces. They never were found in the heathen world. Christ was needed to come from heaven to teach us. Your blessedness is longsuffering, meekness, kindness; your glory is humility before God. The fruit of the Spirit, that He brought from heaven out of the heart of the crucified Christ, and that He gives in our heart, is first and foremost—love.

You know what John says: "No man hath seen God at any time. If we love one another, God dwelleth in us." That is, I cannot see God, but as a compensation I can see my brother, and if I love him God dwells in me. Is that really true? That I cannot see God, but I must love my brother, and God will dwell in me? Loving my brother is the way to real fellowship with God. You know what John further says in that most solemn test, 1 John 4:20: "If a man say, I love God, and hateth his brother, he is a liar; for he that loveth not his brother whom he hath seen, how can he love God whom he hath not seen?" There is a brother, a most unlovable man. He worries you every time you meet him. He is of the very opposite disposition to yours. You are a careful business man, and you have to do with him in your business. He is most untidy, un-businesslike. You say: "I cannot love him."

Oh friend, you have not learned the lesson that Christ wanted to teach above everything. Let a man be what he will, you are to love him. Love is to be the fruit of the Spirit all the day and every day. Yes, listen! if a man loves not his brother whom he hath seen, if you don't love that unlovable man whom you have seen, how can you love God whom you have not seen? You can deceive yourself with beautiful thoughts about loving God. You must prove your love to God by your love to your brother; that is the one standard by which God will judge your love to Him. If the love of God is in your heart you will love your brother. The fruit of the Spirit is love.

And what is the reason that God's Holy Spirit cannot come in power? Is it not possible? You remember the comparison I used in speaking of the vessel. I can dip a little water into a potsherd, a bit of a vessel; but if a vessel is to be full it must be unbroken. And the children of God, wherever they come together, to whatever church or mission or society they belong, must love each other intensely, or the Spirit of God cannot do His work. We talk about grieving the Spirit of God by worldliness and ritualism and formality and error and indifference, but, I tell you, the one thing above everything that grieves God's Spirit is this want of love. Let every heart search itself, and ask that God may search it.

Why are we taught that "the fruit of the Spirit is love"? *Because the Spirit of God has come to make our daily life an exhibition of divine power and a revelation of what God can do for His children.*

In the second and the fourth chapters of Acts we read that the disciples were of one heart and of one soul. During the three years they had walked with Christ they never had been in that spirit. All Christ's teaching could not make them of one heart and one soul. But the Holy Spirit came from heaven and shed the love of God in their hearts, and they were of one heart and one soul. The same Holy Spirit that brought the love of heaven into their hearts must fill us too. Nothing less will do. Even as Christ did, one might preach love for three years with the tongue of an angel, but that would not teach any man to love unless the power of the Holy Spirit should come upon him to bring the love of heaven into his heart.

Think of the Church at large. What divisions! Think of the different bodies. Take the question of holiness, take the question of the cleansing blood, take the question of the baptism of the Spirit—what differences are caused among dear believers by such questions! That there should be differences of opinion does not trouble me. We have not all got the same constitution and temperament and mind. But how often hate, bitterness, contempt, separation, unlovingness, are caused by the holiest truths of God's Word! Our doctrines, our creeds, have been more important than love. We often think we are valiant for the truth, and we forget God's command to speak the truth *in love.* And it was so in the time of the Reformation between the Lutheran and Calvinistic churches. What bitterness there was then in regard to the Holy Supper, which was meant to be the bond of union between all believers! And so, down the ages, the very dearest truths of God have become mountains that have separated us.

If we want to pray in power, and if we want to expect the Holy Spirit to come down in power, and if we want indeed that God shall pour out His Spirit, we must enter into a covenant with God that we love one another with a heavenly love.

Are you ready for that? Only that is true love that is large enough to take in all God's children, the most unloving and unlovable, and unworthy, and unbearable, and trying. If my vow—absolute surrender to God—was true, then it must mean absolute surrender to the divine love to fill me; to be a servant of love, to love every child of God around me. "The fruit of the Spirit is love."

Oh, God did something wonderful when He gave Christ, at His right hand, the Holy Spirit to come down out of the heart of the Father and His everlasting love. And how we have degraded the Holy Spirit into a mere power by which we have to do our work! God forgive us. Oh that the Holy Spirit might be held in honour as a power to fill us with the very life and nature of God and of Christ! "The fruit of the Spirit is love."

I ask once again, Why is it so? And the answer comes: *That is the only power in which Christians really can do their work.* Yes, it is that we need. We want not only love that is to bind us to each other, but we want a divine love in our work for the lost around us. Oh, do we not often undertake a great deal of work just as men undertake work of philanthropy, from a natural spirit of compassion for our fellow men? Do we not often undertake Christian work because our minister or friend calls to it, and do we not often perform Christian work with a certain zeal but without having had a baptism of love?

People often ask: "What is the baptism of fire?" I have answered more than once: I know no fire like the fire of God, the fire of everlasting love that consumed the sacrifice on Calvary. The baptism of love is what the Church needs, and to get that we must begin at once to get down upon our faces before God in confession, and plead: "Lord, let love from heaven flow down into my heart. I am giving up my life to pray and live as one who has given himself up for the everlasting love to dwell in and fill him." Ah yes, if the love of God were in our hearts, what a difference it would make! There are hundreds of believers who say: "I work for Christ, and I feel I could work much more, but I have not the gift. I do not know how or where to begin. I do not know what I can do." Brother, sister, ask God to baptize you with the Spirit of love, and love will find its way. Love is a fire that will burn through every difficulty. You may be a shy, hesitating man, who cannot speak well, but love can burn through everything. God fill us with love! We need it for our work.

You have read many a touching story of love expressed, and you have said, How beautiful! I heard one not long ago. Mrs. Butler had been asked to speak at a Rescue Home where there were a number of poor women. As she arrived there and got to the window with the matron, she saw outside a wretched object sitting, and asked: "Who is that?" The matron answered: "She has been into the house thirty or forty times, and she has always gone away again. Nothing can be done with her, she is so low and hard." But Mrs. Butler said: "She must come in." The matron then said: "We have been waiting for you, and the company is assembled, and you have only an hour for the address."

Mrs. Butler replied: "No, this is of more importance"; and she went outside where the woman was sitting, and said: "My sister, what is the matter?"

"I am not your sister," was the reply.

Then Mrs. Butler laid her hand on her, and said: "Yes, I am your sister, and I love you"; and so she spoke until the heart of the poor woman was touched.

The conversation lasted some time, and the company were waiting patiently. Ultimately Mrs. Butler brought the woman into the room. There was the poor wretched, degraded creature, full of shame. She would not sit on a chair, but sat down on a stool beside the speaker's seat, and she let her lean against her, with her arms around the poor woman's neck, while she spoke to the assembled people. And that love touched the woman's heart; she had found one who really loved her, and that love gave access to the love of Jesus. Praise God! there is love upon earth in the hearts of God's children; but oh, that there were more!

Why is it written, I again ask, that "the fruit of the Spirit is Love"? *Because without love we cannot do our work.* O God, baptize our ministers with a tender love, and our missionaries, and our colporteurs, and our Bible readers, and our workers, and our young men's and young women's associations. Oh that God would begin with us now, and baptize us with heavenly love!

Once again. *It is only love that can fit us for the work of intercession.* I have said that love must fit us for our work. Do you know what the hardest and the most important work is that has to be done for this sinful world? It is the work of intercession, the work of going to God and taking time to lay hold on Him.

A man may be an earnest Christian, an earnest minister, and a man may do good, but alas! how often he has to confess that he knows but little of what it is to tarry with God! May God give us the great gift of an intercessory spirit, a spirit of prayer and supplication! Let me ask you in the name of Jesus not to let a day pass without praying for all saints, and for all God's people.

I find there are Christians who think little of that. I find there are prayer-unions where they pray for the members, and not for all believers. I pray you, take time to pray for the Church of Christ. It is right to pray for the heathen, as I have already said. God help us to pray more for them. It is right to pray for missionaries and for evangelistic work, aid for the unconverted. But Paul did not tell people to pray for the heathen or the unconverted. Paul told them to pray for believers. Do make this your first prayer every day: *Lord, bless Thy saints everywhere.* The state of Christ's Church is indescribably low. Plead for God's people that He would visit them, plead for each other, plead for all believers who are trying to work for God. Let love fill your heart. Ask Christ to pour it out afresh into you every day. Try to get it into you by the Holy Spirit of God: *I am separated unto the Holy Spirit, and the fruit of the Spirit is love.* God help us to understand it.

We have spoken every day at our convention about waiting upon God. May God grant, as the fruit of our convention, that we learn day by day to wait more quietly upon Him. Do not wait upon God only for yourselves, or the power to do so will soon be lost; but give ourselves up to the ministry and the love of intercession, and pray more for God's people, for God's people round about us for the Spirit of love in ourselves and in them, and for the work of God we are connected with; and the answer will surely come, and our waiting upon God will be a source of untold blessing and power. "The fruit of the Spirit is love."

How shall I conclude? I think we must go to God again in intercession. I will ask brethren on the platform to come forward, and we will take up further our supplications, and plead further for the children of God throughout the world, throughout England and Scotland and Ireland, and for the children of God in London who work here in the East End and in this Assembly Hall. Let us plead in faith that God may pour out a spirit of love upon us. Have you a lack of love to confess before God? Then make confession and say before Him: "O Lord, my want of heart, my want of love—I confess it." And then, as you cast that want at His feet, believe that the blood cleanses you, that Jesus comes in His mighty cleansing, saving power to deliver you, and that He will give His Holy Spirit.

"The fruit of the Spirit *is* love."

10

Impossible with Man, Possible with God

"And he said, The things which are impossible with men are possible with God." Luke 18:27

Christ had said to the rich young ruler, "Sell all that thou hast... and come, follow me." The young man went away sorrowful. Christ turned to the disciples, and said: "How hardly shall they that have riches enter into the kingdom of God!" The disciples, we read, were greatly astonished, and answered: "If it is so difficult to enter the kingdom, who, then, can be saved?" And Christ gave this blessed answer: "The things which are impossible with men are possible with God."

We have come to the end of our Convention, and we are now about to part. Our prayers have been offered, time after time; we have listened to God's Word with humiliation and encouragement. And now, how are we to part? I trust this will be a night of faith and confidence, that the Holy Spirit will breathe into our hearts, and that we shall go to our work with one thought—"The things which are impossible with men are possible with God." May God help us to open our ears and hearts to the blessed

Jesus, until He speaks into the very depths of our being—
"the things which are impossible with men are possible
with God."

The text contains just two thoughts—that *in religion, in
the question of salvation and of following Christ by a holy
life, it is impossible for man to do it.* And then alongside
that is the thought—*What is impossible with man is
possible with God.* Let us look at these two sides.

The two thoughts mark the two great lessons that man
has to learn in the religious life. It often takes a long
time to learn the first lesson, that in religion man can do
nothing, that salvation is impossible to man. And often
a man learns that, and yet he does not learn the second
lesson—what has been impossible to him is possible with
God. Blessed is the man who learns both lessons!

The learning of them marks stages in the Christian's
life. The one stage is when a man is trying to do his
utmost and fails, when a man tries to do better and fails
again, when a man tries much more and always fails. And
yet very often he does not even then learn the lesson. *It is
impossible.* Peter spent three years in Christ's school, and
he never learned that word, *It is impossible,* until he had
denied his Lord and went out and wept bitterly. Then he
learned the lesson, *With man it is impossible to serve God
and Christ.*

Just look for a moment at a man who is learning this
lesson, *It is impossible with man.* At first he fights against
it; then he submits to it, but reluctantly and in despair;
at last he accepts it willingly and rejoices in it. At the
beginning of the Christian life the young convert has no
conception of this truth. He has been converted, he has the

joy of the Lord in his heart, he begins to run the race and fight the battle; he is sure he can conquer, for he is earnest and honest, and God will help him. Yet, somehow, very soon he fails where he did not expect it, and sin gets the better of him. He is disappointed; but he thinks: "I was not watchful enough, I did not make my resolutions strong enough." And again he vows, and again he prays, and yet he fails. He thought: "Am I not a regenerate man? Have I not the life of God within me?" And he thinks again: "Yes, and I have Christ to help me, I can live the holy life."

At a later period he comes to another state of mind. He begins to see such a life is impossible, but he does not accept it. There are multitudes of Christians who come to this point: "I cannot"; and then think God never expected them to do what they cannot do. If you tell them that God does expect it, it appears to them a mystery. A good many Christians are living a low life, a life of failure and of sin, instead of rest and victory, because they began to see: "I cannot, it is impossible." And yet they do not understand it fully, and so, under the impression, I cannot, they give way to despair. They will do their best, but they never expect to get on very far.

But God leads His children on to a third stage, when a man comes to take that, *It is impossible,* in its full truth, and yet at the same time says: *"I must do it, and I will do it—it is impossible for man, and yet I must do it"*; when the renewed will begins to exercise its whole power, and in intense longing and prayer begins to cry to God: "Lord, what is the meaning of this?—how am I to be freed from the power of sin?" It is the state of the regenerate man in Romans 7. There you will find the Christian man trying his very utmost to live a holy life. God's law has been revealed to him as reaching down into the very depth of the desires of the heart, and the man can dare to say: "I delight in the law of God after the inward man. To will what is good is present with me. My heart loves the law of God, and my will has chosen that law." Can a man like that fail, with his heart full of delight in God's law and with his will determined to do what is right? Yes. That is what Romans 7 teaches us. There is something more needed. Not only must I delight in the law of God after the inward man, and will what God wills, but I need a divine omnipotence to work it in me. And that is what the apostle Paul teaches in Philippians 2:13: "It is God which worketh in you, both to will and to do."

Note the contrast. In Romans 7, the regenerate man says: "To will is present with me, but to do—I find I cannot do. I will, but I cannot perform." But in Philippians 2, you have a man who has been led on farther, a man who understands that when God has worked the renewed will, God will give the power to accomplish what that will desires. Let us receive this as the first great lesson in the spiritual life: "It is impossible for me, my God; let there be an end of the flesh and all its powers, an end of self, and let it be my glory to be helpless." Praise God for the divine teaching that makes us helpless!

As we used that word yesterday evening—and I cannot let the word go yet —*absolute surrender to God*, were not some of you brought to an end of yourselves, and to feel: I cannot see how I actually can live as a man absolutely surrendered to God every moment of the day—at my table, in my house, in my business, in the midst of trials and temptations? I pray you learn the lesson tonight. If you felt you could not do it, you are on the right road, if you let yourselves be led. Accept that position, and maintain it before God: "My heart's desire and delight, O God, is absolute surrender, but I cannot perform it. It is impossible for me to live that life. It is beyond me." Fall down and learn that when you are utterly helpless, God will come to work in you not only to will, but also to do.

Now comes the second lesson. "The things which *are impossible with men are possible with God.*" I said a little while ago that there is many a man who has learned the lesson, *It is impossible with men*, and then he gives up in helpless despair, and lives a wretched Christian life, without joy, or strength, or victory. And why? Because he does not humble himself to learn that other lesson: *With God all things are possible.*

Your religious life is every day to be a proof that God works impossibilities; your religious life is to be a series of impossibilities made possible and actual by God's almighty power. That is what the Christian needs. He has an almighty God that he worships, and he must learn to understand that he does not need a little of God's power, but he needs—with reverence be it said—the whole of God's omnipotence to keep him right, and to live like a Christian.

The whole of Christianity is a work of God's omnipotence. Look at the birth of Christ Jesus. That was a miracle of divine power, and it was said to Mary: "With God nothing shall be impossible." It was the omnipotence of God. Look at Christ's resurrection. We are taught that it was according to *the exceeding greatness of His mighty power* that God raised Christ from the dead.

Every tree naturally grows on the root from which it springs. An oak tree three hundred years old grows all the time on the one root from which it had its beginning. Christianity had its beginning in the omnipotence of God, and in every soul it must have its continuance in that omnipotence. All the possibilities of the higher Christian life have their origin in a new apprehension of Christ's power to work all God's will in us. I want to call upon you now to come and worship an almighty God. Have you learned to do it? Have you learned to deal so closely with an almighty God that you know omnipotence is working in you? In outward appearance there is often so little sign of it. The apostle Paul said: "I was with you in weakness and in fear and in much trembling, and... my preaching was... in demonstration of the Spirit and of power." From the human side there was feebleness, from the divine side there was divine omnipotence. And that is true of every godly life; and if we would only learn that lesson better, and give a wholehearted, undivided surrender to it, we should learn what blessedness there is in dwelling every hour and every moment with an almighty God.

Have you ever studied in the Bible the attribute of God's omnipotence? You know that it was God's omnipotence that created the world, and created light out of darkness, and created man. But have you studied God's omnipotence in the works of redemption?

Look at Abraham. When God called him to be the father of that people out of which Christ was to be born, God said to him: "I am God Almighty, walk before me and be thou perfect." And God trained Abraham to trust Him as the omnipotent One; and whether it was his going out to a land that he knew not, or his faith as a pilgrim midst the thousands of Canaanites—his faith said: This is my land—or whether it was his faith in waiting twenty-five years for a son in his old age, against all hope, or whether it was the raising up of Isaac from the dead on Mount Moriah when he was going to sacrifice him—Abraham believed God. He was strong in faith, giving glory to God, because he accounted Him who had promised able to perform.

The cause of the weakness of your Christian life is that you want to work it out partly, and to let God help you. And that cannot be. You must come to be utterly helpless, to let God work, and God will work gloriously. It is this that we need if we are indeed to be workers for God. I could go through Scripture and prove to you how Moses, when he led Israel out of Egypt; how Joshua, when he brought them into the land of Canaan; how all God's servants in the Old Testament counted upon the omnipotence of God doing impossibilities. And this God lives today, and this God is the God of every child of His. And yet we are some of us wanting God to give us a little help while we do our best, instead of coming to understand what God wants, and to say: "I can do nothing. God must and will do all." Have you said: "In worship, in work, in sanctification, in obedience to God, I can do nothing of myself, and so my place is to worship the omnipotent God, and to believe that He will work in me every moment"? Oh, may God teach us this! Oh, that God would by His grace show you what a God you have, and to what a God you have entrusted yourself—an omnipotent God, willing with His whole omnipotence to place Himself at the disposal of every child of His! Shall we not take the lesson of the Lord Jesus and say: "Amen; the things which are impossible with men are possible with God"?

Apply that to what we have been dealing with in our Convention. Think of our subject yesterday morning. The Church must be a Church so separated to the Holy Ghost that it has power to separate men unto the Holy Ghost. And every worker must be a worker separated unto the Holy Ghost. We heard that from God's Word. Ah! have any hearts really been expecting from God that that shall be true? Here are in this building, perhaps, one or two thousand workers. Will it be possible that the everlasting God by the Holy Spirit can say of all these workers: They are separated unto the Holy Ghost, and they will live day by day like men and women set apart, not for this mission work or for that mission work, but set apart unto the Holy Ghost? Can we expect in our area, in the Church of Christ, this life will be a reality? "The things which are impossible with men are possible with God." If we fall upon our faces before God in the dust, and say, it *is impossible with men, but with God it is possible*, God will honour our faith.

Remember what we spoke yesterday afternoon about Peter, his self-confidence, self-power, self-will, and how he came to deny his Lord. You feel, "Ah! there is the self-life, there is the flesh-life that rules in me!" And now, have you believed that there is deliverance from that? Have you believed that Almighty God is able so to reveal Christ in your heart, so to let the Holy Spirit rule in you, that the self-life shall not have power or dominion over you? Have you coupled the two together, and with tears of penitence and with deep humiliation and feebleness, cried out: "O God, it is impossible to me; man cannot do it, but, glory to Thy name, it is possible with God"? Have you claimed deliverance? Come and do it tonight. I want you to put yourselves afresh in absolute surrender into the hands of a God of infinite love; and as infinite as His love is His power to do it.

But again. Last night we came to the question of absolute surrender, and felt: That is the want in the Church of Christ, and that is why the Holy Spirit cannot fill us, and why we cannot live as people entirely separated unto the Holy Spirit; that is why the flesh and the self-life cannot be conquered. We have never understood what it is to be absolutely surrendered to God as Jesus was. I know that many a one earnestly and honestly says: "Amen, I accept the message of absolute surrender to God"; and yet thinks: "Will that ever be mine? Can I count upon God to make me one of whom it shall be said in Heaven and on earth and in Hell, he lives in absolute surrender to God?" Brother, sister, "the things which are impossible with men are possible with God." Do believe that when He takes charge of you in Christ, it is possible for God to make you a man of absolute surrender. And God is able to maintain that. He is able to let you rise from bed every morning of the week with that blessed thought directly or indirectly: "I am in God's charge. My God is working out my life for me."

There are some of you weary of thinking about sanctification. You pray, you have longed and cried for it, and yet it appeared so far off! The holiness and humility of

Jesus—you are so conscious of how distant it is. Beloved friends, the one doctrine of sanctification that is scriptural and real and effectual is: "The things which are impossible with men are possible with God." God can sanctify men, and by His almighty and sanctifying power every moment God can keep them. Oh, that we might get a step nearer to our God now! Oh, that the light of God might shine, and that we might know our God better!

And then I could go on to what we said this morning about the life of Christ in us—living like Christ, taking Christ as our Saviour from sin, and as our life and strength. It is God in Heaven who can reveal that in you. What does that prayer of the apostle Paul say: "That he would grant you according to the riches of his glory"—it is sure to be something very wonderful if it is according to the riches of His glory—"to be strengthened with might by his Spirit in the inner man"? Do you not see that it is an omnipotent God working by His omnipotence in the heart of His believing children, so that Christ can become an indwelling Saviour? You have tried to grasp it and to seize it, and you have tried to believe it, and it would not come. It was because you had not been brought to believe that "the things which are impossible with men are possible with God."

And so, coming down to this afternoon, I trust that the word spoken about love may have brought many of us to see: I must have an inflowing of love in quite a new way; my heart must be filled with life from above, from the Fountain of everlasting love, if it is going to overflow all the day; then it will be just as natural for me to love my fellow men as it is natural for the lamb to be gentle and the wolf to be cruel. Until I am brought to such a state that the more a man hates and speaks evil of me, the more unlikable and unlovable a man is, I shall love him all the more; until I am brought to such a state that the more the obstacles and hatred and ingratitude, the more can the power of love triumph in me—until I am brought to see that, I am not saying: "It is impossible with men." But if you have been led to say: "This message has spoken to me about a love utterly beyond my power; it is absolutely impossible"—then we can come to God and say: "It is possible with Thee."

Why is it I speak thus in regard to your spiritual life? For this one reason: A man or a woman who is to work with power for others must know the power of God in his or her own soul. Let every worker, when tonight we close with the earnest prayer: Lord, when we part, let Thy Spirit rest upon every one of us, and not part from us—when we close with that prayer, that every worker, in faith, say: Lord, prove Thy mighty power in my soul, day by day, in such a way that I can show to men that God is almighty to save and to keep.

We want to go out and work. Dear friends, I want you to go out with a joyous face. This great company is to part tonight, alter their different spheres of labour, and we want to bid each other farewell with a heart full of hope and buoyant expectation. Some are crying to God for a great revival. I can say that that is the prayer of my heart unceasingly. Oh, if God would only revive His believing people! I cannot think in the first place of the unconverted formalists of the Church, or of the infidels and sceptics, or of all the wretched and perishing around me, my heart prays in the first place: "My God, revive Thy Church and people." It is not for nothing that there are in thousands of hearts yearnings after holiness and consecration: it is a forerunner of God's power. God works *to will* and then He works *to do*. These yearnings are a witness and a proof that God has worked *to will*. Oh, let us in faith believe that the omnipotent God will work *to do* among His people more than we can ask. "Unto him," Paul said, "who is able to do exceeding abundantly above all that we ask or think... unto him be glory." Let our hearts say that. Glory to God, the omnipotent One, who can do above what we dare to ask or think!

"The things which are impossible with men are possible with God." All around you there is a world of sin and sorrow, and the devil is there. But remember, Christ is on the throne, Christ is stronger, Christ has conquered, and Christ will conquer. Workers, go to your work more humble, and empty, and broken, and helpless, and impotent than ever before. Let us praise God that He can work that in every one of us. But wait on Him. My text casts us down: "The things which are *impossible with men*"; but it ultimately lifts us up high—"are *possible with God*." Get linked to God. Adore and trust Him as the omnipotent One, not only for your own life, but for all the souls that are entrusted to you. Never pray without adoring His omnipotence: and say: *"Mighty God, I claim Thine almightiness."* And the answer to the prayer will come, and like Abraham you will become strong in faith, giving glory to God, because you account Him who hath promised able to perform.

11

"O Wretched Man That I Am!"

"O wretched man that I am! who shall deliver me from the body of this death? I thank God through Jesus Christ our Lord." Romans 7:24, 25

You know the wonderful place that this text has in the wonderful Epistle to the Romans. It stands here at the end of the seventh chapter as the gateway into the eighth. In the first sixteen verses of the eighth chapter the name of the Holy Spirit is found sixteen times; you have there the description and promise of the life that a child of God can live in the power of the Holy Spirit. This begins in the second verse: "The law of the Spirit of life in Christ Jesus hath made me free from the law of sin and death" (Rom. 8:12). From that Paul goes on to speak of the great privileges of the child of God, who is to be led by the Spirit of God. The gateway into all this is in the twenty-fourth verse of the seventh chapter: "O wretched man that I am!" There you have the words of a man who has come to the end of himself. He has in the previous verses described how he had struggled and wrestled in his own power to obey the holy law of God, and had failed. But in answer to his own question he now finds the true answer and cries out: "I thank God through Jesus Christ our Lord." From that he goes on to speak of what that deliverance is that he has found.

I want from these words to describe the path by which a man can be led out of the spirit of bondage into the spirit of liberty. You know how distinctly it is said: "Ye have not received the spirit of bondage again to fear." We are continually warned that this is the great danger of the Christian life, to go again into bondage; and I want to describe the path by which a man can get out of bondage into the glorious liberty of the children of God. Rather, I want to describe the man himself.

First, these words are the language of a *regenerate* man; *second*, of an *impotent* man; *third*, of a *wretched* man; and *fourth*, of a man *on the borders of complete liberty*.

In the first place, then, we have here *the words of a* REGENERATE *man.* You know how much evidence of regeneration from the fourteenth verse of the chapter on to the twenty-third. "It is no more I that do it, but sin that dwelleth in me" (Rom. 7:17): that is the language of a regenerate man, a man who knows that his heart and nature have been renewed, and that sin is now a power in him that is not himself. "I delight in the law of the Lord after the inward man" (Rom. 7:22): that again is the language of a regenerate man. He dares to say when he does evil: "It is no more I that do it, but sin that dwelleth in me." It is of great importance to understand this.

In the first two great sections of the epistle, Paul deals with justification and sanctification. In dealing with justification, he lays the foundation of the doctrine in the teaching about sin, not in the singular, *sin*, but in the plural, *sins*—the actual transgressions. In the second part of the fifth chapter he begins to deal with sin, not as actual transgression, but as a power. Just imagine what a loss it would have been to us if we had not this second half of the seventh chapter of the Epistle to the Romans, if Paul had omitted in his teaching this vital question of the sinfulness of the believer. We should have missed the question we all want answered as to sin in the believer. What is the answer? The regenerate man is one in whom the will has been renewed, and who can say: "I delight in the law of God after the inward man." But,

Secondly, *the regenerate man is also an* IMPOTENT *man.* Here is the great mistake made by many Christian people: they think that when there is a renewed will, it is enough; but that is not the case. This regenerate man tells us: "*I will* to do what is good, but the power *to perform* I find not." How often people tell us that if you set yourself determinedly, you can perform what you will! But this man was as determined as any man can be, and yet he made the confession: "To will is present with me; but how to perform that which is good, I find not" (Rom. 7:18).

But, you ask: "How is it God makes a regenerate man utter such a confession, with a right will, with a heart that longs to do good, and longs to do its very utmost to love God?" Let us look at this question. What has God given us our will for? Had the angels who fell, in their own will, the strength to stand? Surely not. The will of the creature is nothing but an empty vessel in which the power of God is to be made manifest. The creature must seek in God all that it is to be. You have it in the second chapter of the Epistle to the Philippians, and you have it here also, that God's work is to work in us both *to will* and *to do* of His good pleasure. Here is a man who appears to say: "God has not worked *to do* in me." But we are taught that God works both to will and to do. How is the apparent contradiction to be reconciled?

You will find that in this passage (Rom. 7:6–25) the name of the Holy Spirit does not occur once, nor does the name of Christ occur. The man is wrestling and struggling to fulfil God's law. Instead of the Holy Spirit and of Christ, the law is mentioned nearly twenty times. In this chapter, it shows a believer doing his very best to obey the law of God with his regenerate will. Not only this; but you will find the little words, *I*, *me*, *my*, occur more than forty times. It is the regenerate *I* in its impotence seeking to obey the law without being filled with the Spirit. This is the experience of almost every saint. After conversion a man begins to do his best, and he fails; but if we are brought into the full light, we need fail no longer. Nor need we fail at all if we have received the Spirit in His fullness at conversion.

God allows that failure that the regenerate man should be taught his own utter impotence. It is in the course of this struggle that there comes to us this sense of our utter sinfulness. It is God's way of dealing with us. He allows that man to strive to fulfil the law that, as he strives and wrestles, he may be brought to this: "I am a regenerate child of God, but I am utterly helpless to obey His law." See what strong words are used all through the chapter to describe this condition: "I am carnal, sold under sin" (Rom. 7:14); "I see another law in my members bringing me into captivity" (Rom. 7:23); and last of all, "O wretched man that I am! who shall deliver me from the body of this death?" (Rom. 7:24). This believer who bows here in deep contrition is utterly unable to obey the law of God. But,

Thirdly, *not only is the man who makes this confession a regenerate and an impotent man, but he is also a* WRETCHED *man.* He is utterly unhappy and miserable; and what is it that makes him so utterly miserable? It is because God has given him a nature that loves Himself. He is deeply wretched because he feels he is not obeying his God. He says, with brokenness of heart: "It is not I that do it, but I am under the awful power of sin, which is holding me down. It is I, and yet not I: alas! alas! it is myself; so closely am I bound up with it, and so closely is it intertwined with my very nature." Blessed be God when a man learns to say: "O wretched man that I am!" from the depth of his heart. He is on the way to the eighth chapter of Romans.

There are many who make this confession a pillow for sin. They say that if Paul had to confess his weakness and helplessness in this way, what are they that they should try to do better? So the call to holiness is quietly set aside. Would God that every one of us had learned to say these words in the very spirit in which they are written here! When we hear sin spoken of as the abominable thing that God hates, do not many of us wince before the word? Would that all Christians who go on sinning and sinning would take this verse to heart. If ever you utter a sharp word say: "O wretched man that I am!" And every time you lose your temper, kneel down and understand that it never was meant by God that this was to be the state in which His child should remain. Would God that we would take this word into our daily life, and say it every time we are touched about our own honour, and every time we say sharp things, and every time we sin against the Lord God, and against the Lord Jesus Christ in His humility, and in His obedience, and in His self-sacrifice! Would to God you could forget everything else, and cry out: "O wretched man that I am! who shall deliver me from the body of this death?" Why should you say this whenever you commit sin? Because it is when a man is brought to this confession that deliverance is at hand.

And remember it was not only the sense of being impotent and taken captive that made him wretched, but it was above all the sense of sinning against his God. The law was doing its work, making sin *exceedingly sinful* in his sight. The thought of continually grieving God became utterly unbearable—it was this that brought forth the piercing cry: "O wretched man!" As long as we talk and reason about our impotence and our failure, and only try to find out what Romans 7 means, it will profit us but little; but when once *every sin* gives new intensity to the sense of wretchedness, and we feel our whole state as one of not only helplessness, but actual exceeding sinfulness, we shall be pressed not only to ask: "Who shall deliver us?" but to cry: "I thank God through Jesus Christ my Lord."

Fourthly, *when a man comes here he is on the very brink of deliverance.* The man has tried to obey the beautiful law of God. He has loved it, he has wept over his sin, he has tried to conquer, he has tried to overcome fault after fault, but every time he has ended in failure. What did he mean by "the body of this death"? Did he mean, my body when I die? Surely not. In the eighth chapter you have the answer to this question in the words: "If ye through the Spirit do mortify the deeds of the body, ye shall live." *That* is the body of death from which he is seeking deliverance. And now he is on the brink of deliverance! In the twenty-third verse of the seventh chapter we have the words: "I see another law in my members, warring against the law of my mind, and bringing me into *captivity* to the law of sin which is in my members." It is a *captive* that cries: "O wretched man that I am! who shall deliver me from the body of this death?" He is a man who feels himself bound. But look to the contrast in the second verse of the eighth chapter: "The law of the Spirit of life in Christ Jesus hath *made me free* from the law of sin and death." That is the deliverance through Jesus Christ our Lord; the *liberty* to the captive which the Spirit brings. Can you keep captive any longer a man made free by the "law of the Spirit of life in Christ Jesus"?

But you say, the regenerate man, had not he the Spirit of Jesus when he spoke in the sixth chapter?

Yes, *but he did not know what the Holy Spirit could do for him.* God does not work by His Spirit as He works by a blind force in nature. He leads His people on as reasonable, intelligent beings, and therefore when He wants to give us that Holy Spirit whom He has promised, He brings us first to the end of self, to the conviction that though we have been striving to obey the law, we have failed. When we have come to the end of that, then He shows us that in the Holy Spirit we have the power of obedience, the power of victory, and the power of real holiness.

God works *to will*, and He is ready to work *to do*, but,

alas! many Christians misunderstand this. They think because they have the will, it is enough, and that now they are able to do. This is not so. The new will is a permanent gift, an attribute of the new nature. The power to do is not a permanent gift, but must be each moment received from the Holy Spirit. It is the man who is conscious *of his own impotence as a believer* who will learn that by the Holy Spirit *he can live a holy life.* This man is on the brink of that great deliverance; the way has been prepared for the glorious eighth chapter.

I now come to you this evening with the solemn thought: Where are you living? Is it with you, "O wretched man that I am! who shall deliver me?" with now and then a little experience of the power of the Holy Spirit? or is it, "I thank God through Jesus Christ! The law of the Spirit hath set me free from the law of sin and of death"?

What the Holy Spirit does is to give the victory. "If ye through the Spirit do mortify the deeds of the flesh, ye shall live" (Rom. 8:13). It is the Holy Ghost who does this—the third Person of the Godhead. He it is who, when the heart is opened wide to receive Him, comes in and reigns there, and mortifies the deeds of the body, day by day, hour by hour, and moment by moment.

I want to bring this to a point. Remember, dear friends, that if our Convention is to do any good, its object is to come to decision and action. There are in Scripture two very different sorts of Christians. The Bible speaks in *Romans, Corinthians* and *Galatians* about yielding to the flesh; and that is the life of tens of thousands of believers. All their want of joy in the Holy Ghost, and their lack of the liberty He gives, is just owing to the flesh. The Spirit is within them, but the flesh rules the life. To be led by the Spirit of God is what they need. Would God that I could make every child of His realize what it means that the everlasting God has given His dear Son, Christ Jesus, to watch over you every day, and that what you have to do is to trust; and that the work of the Holy Spirit is to enable you every moment to remember Jesus, and to trust Him! The Spirit has come to keep the link with Him unbroken every moment. Praise God for the Holy Spirit! We are so accustomed to think of the Holy Spirit as a luxury, for special times, or for special ministers and men. But the Holy Spirit is necessary for every believer, every moment of the day. Praise God you have Him, and that He gives you the full experience of the deliverance in Christ, as He makes you free from the power of sin.

Who longs to have the power and the liberty of the Holy Spirit? Oh, brother, bow before God in one final cry of despair: "O God, must I go on sinning this way forever? Who shall deliver me, O wretched man that I am! from the body of this death?" Are you ready to sink before God in that cry and seek the power of Jesus to dwell and work in you? Are you ready to say: "I thank God through Jesus Christ"?

What good does it do that we go to church or attend conventions, that we study our Bibles and pray, unless our lives are filled with the Holy Spirit? That is what God wants; and nothing else will enable us to live a life of power and peace. You know that when a minister or parent is using the catechism, when a question is asked an answer is expected. Alas! how many Christians are content with the question put here: "O wretched man that am! who ... deliver me from the body of this death?" ... never ... answer. Instead of answering, they are silent. Instead, saying: "I thank God through Jesus Christ our Lord." ... there forever repeating the question without ... If ... want the path to the full deliverance of Christ, and the liberty of the Spirit, the glorious liberty of the children of God, take it through the seventh chapter of Romans; and then say: "I thank God through Jesus Christ our Lord." Be not content to remain ever groaning, but say: "I, a wretched man, thank God, through Jesus Christ. Even though I do not see it all, I am going to praise God."

There is deliverance, there is the liberty of the Holy Spirit. The kingdom of God is "joy in the Holy Ghost" (Rom. 14:17).

12

"Having Begun in the Spirit"

The word from which I wish to address you, you will find in the Epistle to the Galatians, the third chapter, at the third verse; let us read the second verse also: *"This only would I learn of you, received ye the Spirit by the works of the law, or by the hearing of faith? Are ye so foolish?"* And then comes my text, *"Having begun in the Spirit, are ye now made perfect by the flesh?"*

When we speak of the quickening or the deepening or the strengthening of the spiritual life, we are thinking of something that is feeble and wrong and sinful; and it is a great thing to take our place this evening before God with the confession: O God, our spiritual life is not what it should be! May God work that in every heart.

As we look round about on the Church we see so many indications of feebleness, and failure, and of sin, and of shortcoming, that we are compelled to ask, Why is it? Is there any necessity for the Church of Christ to be living in such a low state? Or is it actually possible that God's people should be living always in the joy and strength of their God? Every believing heart must answer, It is possible.

Then comes the great question, Why is it, how is it

to be accounted for, that God's Church as a whole is so feeble, and that the great majority of Christians are not living up to their privileges? There must be a reason for it. Has God not given Christ His Almighty Son to be the Keeper of every believer, to make Christ an ever present reality, and to impart and communicate to us all that we have in Christ? God has given His Son, and God has given His Spirit. How is it that believers do not live up to their privileges?

We find in more than one of the Epistles a very solemn answer to that question. There are Epistles, such as the First to the Thessalonians where Paul writes to the Christians in effect: I want you to grow, to abound, to increase more and more. They were young, and there were things lacking in their faith, but their state was so far satisfactory, and gave him great joy, and he writes time after time: I pray God that you may abound more and more; I write to you to increase more and more. But there are other Epistles where he takes a very different tone, especially the Epistles to the Corinthians and the Galatians, and he tells them in many different ways what the one reason was, that they were not living as Christians ought to live; many were under the power of the flesh. My text is one example. He reminds them that by the preaching of faith they had received the Holy Spirit. He had preached Christ to them; they had accepted that Christ, and had received the Holy Spirit in power. But what happened? Having begun in the Spirit, they tried to perfect the work that the Spirit had begun, in the flesh by their own effort. We find the same teaching in the Epistles to the Corinthians.

Now we have here a solemn discovery of what the great

want is in the Church of Christ. God has called the Church of Christ to live in the power of the Holy Spirit and the Church is living for the most part in the power of human flesh, and of will and energy and effort apart from the Spirit of God. I doubt not that that is the case with many individual believers; and oh, if God will use me to give you a message from Him, my one message will be this: If the Church will return to acknowledge that the Holy Spirit is her strength and her help, and if the Church will return to give up everything, and wait upon God to be filled with the Spirit, her days of beauty and gladness will return, and we shall see the glory of God revealed amongst us. This is my message to every individual believer: Nothing will help you unless you come to understand, I must live every day under the power of the Holy Ghost. God wants you to be a living vessel in whom the power of the Spirit is to be manifested every hour and every moment of your life, and God will enable you to be that.

Now let us try and learn what this word to the Galatians teaches us—some very simple thoughts. It shows us how *the beginning of the Christian life is receiving the Holy Spirit*. It shows us *what great danger there is of forgetting that we are to live by the Spirit*, and not live after the flesh. It shows us what *the fruits and the proofs are of our seeking perfection in the flesh*. And then it suggests to us *the way of deliverance from this state*.

First of all, Paul says, *"Having begun in the Spirit."* Remember, the Apostle not only preached justification by faith, but he preached something more. He preached this—the Epistle is full of it—that justified men cannot live but by the Holy Spirit, and that therefore God gives to every justified man the Holy Spirit to seal him. The Apostle says to them in effect more than once: How did you receive the Holy Spirit? Was it by the preaching of the law, or by the preaching of faith? He could point back to that time when there had been a mighty revival under his teaching. The power of God had been manifested, and the Galatians were compelled to confess: Yes, we have got the Holy Ghost: accepting Christ by faith, by faith we received the Holy Spirit.

Now, it is to be feared that there are many Christians who hardly know that when they believed they received the Holy Ghost. A great many Christians can say: I received pardon and I received peace. But if you were to ask them, have you received the Holy Ghost? They would hesitate, and many, if they were to say, Yes, would say it with hesitation; and they would tell you that they hardly knew what it was, since that time, to walk in the power of the Holy Spirit. Let us try and take hold of this great truth: the beginning of the true Christian life is to receive the Holy Ghost. And the work of every Christian minister is what was the work of St. Paul—to remind his people: Christians, you received the Holy Ghost, and you must live according to His guidance, and you must live in his power.

If those Galatians who received the Holy Spirit in power were tempted to go astray by that terrible danger of perfecting in the flesh what had been begun in the Spirit, how much more danger do those Christians run who hardly ever know that they have received the Holy Spirit, or who, if they know it as a matter of belief, hardly ever think of it and hardly ever praise God for it!

If we are asking in earnest tonight, What is to be done to have Christ's Church restored? Let us at once accept the truth that the Holy Ghost must be far more honoured. In every believer there must be a deep, abiding conviction: What I got from God was not only pardon in heaven, but the Holy Spirit within my heart, to live there and to be my strength.

But now look, in the second place, at *the great danger*. You all know what shunting is on a railway. A locomotive with its train may be run in a certain direction, and the points at some place may not be properly opened or closed, and unobservingly it is shunted off to the right or to the left. And if that takes place, for instance, on a dark night, the train goes in the wrong direction, and the people might never know it until they have gone some distance.

And just so God gives Christians the Holy Spirit with this intention, that every day all their life should be lived in the power of the Spirit. A man cannot live one hour a godly life unless by the power of the Holy Ghost. He may live a proper, consistent life, as people call it, an irreproachable life, a life of virtue and diligent service; but to live a life acceptable to God, in the enjoyment of God's salvation and God's love, to live and walk in the power of the new life he cannot do it unless he be guided by the Holy Spirit every day and every hour.

But now listen to the danger. The Galatians received the Holy Ghost, but what was begun by the Spirit they tried to perfect in the flesh. How? They fell back again under Judaising teachers who told them they must be circumcised. They began to seek their religion in external observances. And so Paul uses that expression about those teachers who had them circumcised, that *they sought to glory in their flesh.*

You sometimes hear the expressions used, *religious flesh.* What is meant by that? It is simply an expression made to give utterance to this thought: My human nature and my human will and my human effort can be very active in religion, and after being converted, and after receiving the Holy Ghost, I may begin in my own strength to try to serve God. I may be very diligent and doing a great deal, and yet all the time it is more the work of human flesh than of God's Spirit. What a solemn thought, that man can, without noticing it, be shunted off from the line of the Holy Ghost on to the line of the flesh; that he can be most diligent and make great sacrifices, and yet it is all in the power of the human will! Ah, the great question for us to ask of God in self-examination is, that we may be shown whether our religious life is lived more in the power of the flesh than in the power of the Holy Spirit. A man may be a preacher, he may work most diligently in his ministry, a man may be a Christian worker, and others may tell of him that he makes great sacrifices, and yet you can feel there is a want about it. You feel that he is not a spiritual man; there is no spirituality about his life. How many Christians there are about whom no one would ever think of saying, What a spiritual man he is! Ah! There is the weakness of the Church of Christ. It is all in that one word—*flesh.*

Now, the flesh may manifest itself in many ways. It may be manifested in fleshly wisdom. My mind may be most active about religion, I may preach or write or think or meditate, and delight in being occupied with things in

God's Book and in God's Kingdom; and yet the power of the Holy Ghost may be markedly absent. I fear that if you take the preaching throughout the Church of Christ in England and Scotland and Holland and Europe and the United States, and you ask the question, Why is there, alas! so little converting power in the preaching of the word? Why is it that there is so much work and often so little result for eternity? And if you ask the further question, Why is it that the Word has so little power to build up believers in holiness and in consecration? The answer will come: It is the absence of the power of the Holy Ghost. And why is this? There can be no other reason but that the flesh and human energy have taken the place that the Holy Ghost ought to have. That was true of the Galatians, it was true of the Corinthians. You know Paul said to them: I cannot speak to you as to spiritual men; you ought to be spiritual men, but you are carnal. And you know how often in the course of his Epistles he had to reprove and condemn them for strife and for divisions.

A third thought: *What are the proofs or indications that a church like the Galatians, or a Christian is serving God in the power of the flesh—is perfecting in the flesh what was begun in the Spirit?* The answer is very easy. Religious self-effort always ends in sinful flesh. What was the state of those Galatians? Striving to be justified by the works of the law. And yet they were quarrelling and in danger of devouring one another. Count up the expressions that the Apostle uses to indicate their want of love, and you will find more than twelve—envy, jealousy, bitterness, strife, and all sorts of expressions. Read in the fourth and fifth chapters what he says about that. You see how they tried to serve God in their own strength, and they failed utterly. All this religious effort resulted in failure; the power of sin and the sinful flesh got the better of them, and their whole condition was one of the saddest that could be thought of.

This comes to us with unspeakable solemnity. There is a complaint everywhere in the Christian Church of the want of a high standard of integrity and godliness, even among the professing members of Christian churches. I remember a sermon which I heard preached by Dr. Dykes, in this church, on commercial morality, and he spoke of what was to be found in London. And oh, if we speak not only of the commercial morality or immorality that is to be found in London, but if we go into the homes of Christians, and if we think of the life to which God has called His children, and which He enables them to live by the Holy Ghost, and if we think of how much, nevertheless, there is of unlovingness and temper and sharpness and bitterness, and if we think how much there is very often of strife amongst the members of churches, and how much there is of envy and jealousy and sensitiveness and pride, then we are compelled to say: Where are the marks of the presence of the Spirit of the Lamb of God? Wanting, sadly wanting!

Many people speak of these things as though they were the natural result of our feebleness, and cannot well be helped. Many people speak of these things as sins, yet have given up the hope of conquering them. Many people speak of these things in the Church around them, and do not see the least prospect of ever having the things changed. There is no prospect until there comes a radical change, until the Church of God begins to see that every sin in the believer comes from the flesh, from a fleshly life amidst our religious activities, from a striving in self-effort to serve God. Until we learn to make confession, and until we begin to see we must somehow or other get God's Spirit in power back to His Church, we must fail. Where did the Church begin in Pentecost? There they began in the Spirit. But, alas, how the church of the next century went off into the flesh! They thought to perfect the Church in the flesh.

Do not let us think, because the blessed Reformation restored the great doctrine of justification by faith, that the power of the Holy Spirit was then fully restored. If it is our faith that God is going to have mercy on His Church in these last ages, it will be because the doctrine and the truth about the Holy Spirit will not only be studied, but sought after with a whole heart; and not only because that truth will be sought after, but because ministers and congregations will be found bowing before God in deep abasement with one cry: We have grieved God's Spirit; we have tried to be Christian churches with as little as possible of God's Spirit; we have not sought to be churches filled with the Holy Ghost. Did you hear that awful indictment that God's servant who spoke before me brought against the Church of Christ, when he said that all the feebleness in the Church is owing to the refusal of the Church to obey its God? Is not that an awful thing to say? The Church redeemed by the blood of Christ, the Church baptized by the Holy Ghost, refusing to obey God! And yet it is so.

And why is it so? I know your answer. You say: We

are too feeble and too helpless, and we try to obey, and we vow to obey, but somehow we fail. Ah, yes; *you fail because you do not accept the strength of God*. God alone can work out His will in you. You cannot work out God's will, but His Holy Spirit can; and until the Church, until believers grasp this, and cease trying by human effort to do God's will, and wait upon the Holy Spirit to come with all His omnipotent and enabling power, the Church will never be what God wants her to be, and what God is willing to make of her.

I come now to my last thought, the question, *What is the way to restoration?* Beloved friends, the answer is simple and easy. If that train has been shunted off, there is nothing for it but to come back to the point at which it was led away. The Galatians had no other way in returning but to come back to where they had gone wrong, to come back from all religious effort in their own strength, and from seeking anything by their own work, and to yield themselves humbly to the Holy Spirit. There is no other way for us as individuals. Is there any brother or sister here whose heart is conscious: Alas! my life knows but little of the power of the Holy Ghost? I come to you with God's message, that just as truly as the everlasting Son of God came to this world and wrought His wonderful works, that just as truly as on Calvary He died and wrought out your redemption by His precious blood, so, just as truly, can the Holy Spirit come into your heart, that with His Divine Power He may sanctify you and enable you to do God's blessed will, and fill your hearts with joy and with strength. But alas! We have forgotten, we have grieved, we have dishonoured the Holy Spirit, and He has not been able to do His work. But I bring you the message: The Father in Heaven loves to fill His children with His Holy Spirit. God longs to give each one of you individually, separately, the power of the Holy Spirit for your daily life. The command comes to us individually, unitedly. God wants us as His children to arise and place our sins before Him, and to call upon Him for mercy. Oh, are ye so foolish, having begun in the Spirit, are ye perfecting in the flesh that which was begun in the Spirit? Let us bow in shame, and confess before God how our fleshly religion, our self-effort, and self-confidence, have been the cause of every failure.

I have often been asked by young Christians: Why is it that I fail so? I did so solemnly vow with my whole heart, and did desire to serve God; why have I failed? To such I always give the one answer: My dear friend, you are trying to do in your own strength what Christ alone can do in you. And when they tell me: I am sure I knew Christ alone could do it, I was not trusting in myself, my answer always is: You were trusting in yourself or you could not have failed. If you had trusted Christ, He could not fail. Oh, this perfecting in the flesh what was begun in the Spirit runs far deeper through us than we know. Let us ask God to discover to us that it is only when we are brought to utter shame and emptiness that we shall be prepared to receive the blessing that comes from on high.

And so I come tonight with these two questions. Are you living, beloved brother minister—I ask it of every minister of the Gospel—are you living under the power of the Holy Ghost? Are you living as an anointed, Spirit-filled man in your ministry and your life before God?

O brethren, our place is an awful one. We have to show people what God will do for us, not in our words and teaching, but in our life. God help us to do it! I ask it of every member of Christ's Church and of every believer: Are you living a life under the power of the Holy Spirit day by day, or are you attempting to live without that? Remember you cannot. Are you consecrated, given up to the Spirit to work in you and to live in you? Oh, come and confess every failure of temper, every failure of tongue however small, every failure owing to the absence of the Holy Spirit and the presence of the power of self. Are you consecrated, are you given up to the Holy Spirit?

If your answer be *No*, then I come with a second question—Are you willing to be consecrated? Are you willing to give up yourself to the power of the Holy Spirit?

You know very well, I trust, that the human side of consecration will not help you. I may consecrate myself a hundred times with all the intensity of my being, and that will not help me. What will help me is this—that God from heaven accepts and seals the consecration.

And now are you willing to give yourselves up to the Holy Spirit? You can do it tonight. A great deal may still be dark and dim, and beyond what we understand, and you may feel nothing; but come. Tonight we want to go into God's presence, and to feel that for tomorrow, and the next day, and the next, we want to meet God Himself. God alone can affect the change. God alone, who gave us the Holy Spirit, can restore the Holy Spirit in power into our life. God alone can "strengthen us with might by His Spirit in the inner man." All you who have been praying for God's blessing on our conference, look to God this evening, and say: O God, if Thou art not with us, nothing will help us. Except God be here, you might have meetings for a month, and they might cause a little quickening and awakening, but they will not help you permanently. But God will help us if we cast ourselves in helplessness before Him. Oh, let us do so. Tonight let us ask God, and during these three days, that in His great mercy He would visit our souls. Let us, meeting by meeting, step by step, plead with Him: Lord, come and visit Thy Church and Thy people, and let the power of the Holy Spirit be manifested among us. And let us, in prospect of that, and with the expectation of that, even now say: Lord, I claim for myself, and I claim for my fellow-Christians, and I claim for this Conference, the presence and the power of the Holy Spirit. And to every waiting heart that will make the sacrifice, and give up everything, and give time to cry and pray to God, the answer will come. The blessing is not far off. Our God delights to help us. He will enable us to perfect, not in the flesh, but in the Spirit, what was begun in the Spirit.

13

"Kept By the Power of God"

The words from which I wish to speak, you will find in 1 Peter 1:5. The third, fourth and fifth verses are: *"Blessed be the God and Father of our Lord Jesus Christ, which... hath begotten us again unto a lively hope by the resurrection of Jesus Christ from the dead, to an inheritance incorruptible... reserved in heaven for you,"* (and the fifth verse) *"who are kept by the power of God through faith unto salvation."* The words of my text are: *"Kept by the power of God through faith."*

There we have two wonderful, blessed truths about the keeping by which a believer is kept unto salvation. One truth is, *Kept by the power of God*; and the other truth is, *Kept through faith*. We want to look at the two sides—at God's side and His almighty power, offered to us to be our Keeper every moment of the day; and at the human side, we having nothing to do but in faith to let God do His keeping work. We are begotten again to an inheritance kept in Heaven for us; and we are kept here on earth by the power of God. We see there is a double keeping—*the inheritance kept for me* in Heaven, and *I on earth kept for the inheritance* there.

Now, as to the first part of this keeping, there is no doubt and no question. God keeps the inheritance in Heaven very wonderfully and perfectly, and it is waiting there safely. And the same God keeps me for the inheritance. That is what I want to understand.

You know it is very foolish of a father to take great trouble to have an inheritance for his children, and to keep it for them, if he does not keep them for it. What would you think of a man spending his whole time and making every sacrifice to amass money, and as he gets his tens of thousands, you ask him why it is that he sacrifices himself so, and his answer is: "I want to leave my children a large inheritance, and I am keeping it for them"—if you were then to hear that that man takes no trouble to educate his children, that he allows them to run upon the street wild, and to go on in paths of sin and ignorance and folly, what would you think of him? Would not you say: "Poor man! he is keeping an inheritance for his children, but he is not keeping or preparing his children for the inheritance"! And there are so many Christians who think: "My God is keeping the inheritance for me"; but they cannot believe: "My God is keeping me for that inheritance." The same power, the same love, the same God doing the double work.

Now, I want to speak about a work God does upon us— keeping us for the inheritance. I have already said that we have two very simple truths: the one the divine side—*we are kept by the power of God*; the other, the human side— *we are kept through faith*.

First, look at the divine side—*kept by the power of God*.

Think, first of all, that *this keeping is all-inclusive*. What is kept? *You* are kept. How much of you? The whole being. Does God keep one part of you and not another? No. Some people have an idea that this is a sort of vague, general keeping, and that God will keep them in such a way that when they die they will get to Heaven. But they do not apply that word *kept* to everything in their being and nature. And yet that is what God wants. Here I have a watch. Suppose that this watch had been borrowed from a friend, and he said to me: "When you go to Europe, I will let you take it with you, but mind you keep it safely and bring it back." And suppose I damaged the watch, and had the hands broken, and the face defaced, and some of the wheels and springs spoiled, and took it back in that condition, and handed it to my friend; he would say: "Ah, but I gave you that watch on condition that you would keep it."

"Have I not kept it? There is the watch."

"But I did not want you to keep it in that general way, so that you should bring me back only the shell of the watch, or the remains. I expected you to keep every part of it." And so God does not want to keep us in this general way, so that at the last, somehow or other, we shall be saved as by fire, and just get into Heaven. But the keeping power and the love of God applies to every particular of our being.

There are some people who think God will keep them in spiritual things, but not in temporal things. This latter, they say, lies outside of His line. Now, God sends you to work in the world, but He did not say: "I must now leave you to go and earn your own money, and to get your livelihood for yourself." He knows you are not able to keep yourself. But God says: "My child, there is no work you are to do, and no business in which you are engaged, and not a cent which you are to spend, but I, your Father, will take that up into my keeping." God not only cares for the spiritual, but for the temporal also. The greater part of the life of many people must be spent, sometimes eight or nine or ten hours a day, amid the temptations and distractions of business; but God will care for you there. The keeping of God includes all.

There are other people who think: "Ah! in time of trial God keeps me, but in times of prosperity I do not need His keeping; then I forget Him and let Him go." Others, again, think the very opposite. They think: "In time of prosperity, when things are smooth and quiet, I am able to cling to God, but when heavy trials come, somehow or other my will rebels, and God does not keep me then." Now, I bring you the message that in prosperity as in adversity, in the sunshine as in the dark, your God is ready to keep you all the time. Then again, there are others who think of this keeping thus: "God will keep me from doing very great wickedness, but there are small sins I cannot expect God to keep me from. There is the sin of temper. I cannot expect God to conquer that." When you hear of some man who has been tempted and gone astray or fallen into drunkenness or murder, you thank God for His keeping power. "I might have done the same as that man," you say, "if God had not kept me." And you believe He kept you from drunkenness and murder. And why do you not need believe that God can keep you from outbreaks of temper? You thought that this was of less importance; you did not remember that the great commandment of the New Testament is—"Love one another as I have loved you."

And when your temper and hasty judgment and sharp words came out, you sinned against the highest law—the law of God's love. And yet you say: "God will not, God cannot"—no, you will not say, God cannot; but you say, "God does not keep me from that." You perhaps say: "He can; but there is something in me that cannot attain to it, and which God does not take away."

I want to come to you this morning and ask you, Can believers live a holier life than is generally lived? Can believers experience the keeping power of God all the day, to keep them from sin? Can believers be kept in fellowship with God? And I bring you a message from the Word of God, in these words: *Kept by the power of God.* There is no qualifying clause to them. The meaning is, that if you will entrust yourself entirely and absolutely to the omnipotence of God, He will delight to keep you.

Some people think that they never can get so far as that every word of their mouth should be to the glory of God. But it is what God wants of them, it is what God expects of them. God is willing to set a watch at the door of their mouth, and if God will do that, cannot He keep their tongue and their lips? He can; and that is what God is going to do for them that trust Him. God's keeping is all-inclusive, and let everyone who longs to live a holy life think out all their needs, and all their weaknesses, and all their shortcomings, and all their sins, and say deliberately: "Is there any sin that my God cannot keep me from?" And the heart will have to answer: "No; God can keep me from every sin."

Secondly, if you want to understand this keeping, remember that it is not only an all-inclusive keeping, but it is an *almighty keeping*. I want to get that truth burned into my soul; I want to worship God until my whole heart is filled with the thought of His omnipotence. God is almighty, and the Almighty God offers Himself to work in my heart, to do the work of keeping me; and I want to get linked with Omnipotence, or rather, linked to the Omnipotent One, to the living God, and to have my place in the hollow of His hand. You read the Psalms, and you think of the wonderful thoughts in many of the expressions that David uses; as, for instance, when he speaks about God being *our God, our Fortress, our Refuge, our strong Tower, our Strength* and *our Salvation*. David had very wonderful views of how the everlasting God is Himself the hiding place of the believing soul, and of how He takes the believer and keeps him in the very hollow of His hand, in the secret of His pavilion, under the shadow of His wings, under His very feathers. And there David lived. And oh, we who are the children of Pentecost, we who have known Christ and His blood and the Holy Ghost sent down from Heaven, why is it we know so little of what it is to walk tremblingly step by step with the Almighty God as our Keeper?

Have you ever thought that in every action of grace in your heart you have the whole omnipotence of God engaged to bless you? When I come to a man and he bestows upon me a gift of money, say £100, I get it and go away with it. He has given me something of his; the rest he keeps for himself. But that is not the way with the power of God. God can part with nothing of His own power, and therefore I can experience the power and goodness of God only so far as I am in contact and fellowship with

Himself; and when I come into contact and fellowship with Himself, I come into contact and fellowship with the whole omnipotence of God, and have the omnipotence of God to help me every day. A son has, perhaps, a very rich father, and as the former is about to commence business the father says: "You can have as much money as you want for your undertaking." All the father has is at the disposal of the son. And that is the way with God, your Almighty God. You can hardly take it in; you feel yourself such a little worm. His omnipotence needed to keep a little worm! Yes, His omnipotence is needed to keep every little worm that lives in the dust, and also to keep the universe, and therefore His omnipotence is much more needed in keeping your soul and mine from the power of sin.

Oh, if you want to grow in grace, do learn to begin here. In all your judgings and meditations and thoughts and deeds and questionings and studies and prayers, learn to be kept by your Almighty God. What is Almighty God not going to do for the child that trusts Him? The Bible says: "Above all that we can ask or think." It is Omnipotence you must learn to know and trust, and then you will live as a Christian ought to live. How little we have learned to study God, and to understand that a godly life is a life full of God, a life that loves God and waits on Him, and trusts Him, and allows Him to bless it! We cannot do the will of God except by the power of God. God gives us the first experience of His power to prepare us to long for more, and to come and claim all that He can do. God help us to trust Him every day.

Another thought. *This keeping is* not only all-inclusive and omnipotent, but also *continuous and unbroken.*

People sometimes say: "For a week or a month God has kept me very wonderfully: I have lived in the light of His countenance, and I cannot say what joy I have not had in fellowship with Him. He has blessed me in my work for others. He has given me souls, and at times I felt as if I were carried heavenward on eagle wings. But it did not continue. It was too good; it could not last." And some say: "It was necessary that I should fall to keep me humble." And others say: "I know it was my own fault; but somehow you cannot always live up in the heights."

Oh, beloved, why is it? Can there be any reason why the keeping of God should not be continuous and unbroken? Just think. All life is in unbroken continuity. If my life were stopped for half an hour I would be dead, and my life gone. Life is a continuous thing, and the life of God is the life of His Church, and the life of God is His almighty power working in us. And God comes to us as the Almighty One, and without any condition He offers to be my Keeper, and His keeping means that day by day, moment by moment, God is going to keep us.

If I were to ask you the question: "Do you think God is able to keep you one day from actual transgression?" you would answer: "I not only know He is able to do it, but I think He has done it. There have been days in which He has kept my heart in His holy presence, when, though I have always had a sinful nature within me, He has kept me from conscious, actual transgression."

Now, if He can do that for an hour or a day, why not for two days? Oh! let us make God's omnipotence as revealed in His Word the measure of our expectations. Has God not said in His Word: "I, the Lord, do keep it, and will water it every moment"? What can that mean? Does "every moment" mean every moment? Did God promise of that vineyard of red wine that *every moment* He would water it so that the heat of the sun and the scorching wind might never dry it up? Yes. In South Africa they sometimes make a graft, and above it they tie a bottle of water, so that now and then there shall be a drop to saturate what they have put about it. And so the moisture is kept there unceasingly until the graft has had time to stroke, and resist the heat of the sun.

Will our God, in His tender hearted love toward us, not keep us every moment when He has promised to do so? Oh! if we once got hold of the thought: Our whole religious life is to be God's doing—"It is God that worketh in us to will and to do of his good pleasure"—when once we get faith to expect that from God, God will do all for us.

The keeping is to be continuous. Every morning God will meet you as you wake. It is not a question: If I forgot to wake in the morning with the thought of Him, what will come of it? If you trust your waking to God, God will meet you in the morning as you wake with His divine sunshine and love, and He will give you the consciousness that through the day you have got God to take charge of you continuously with His almighty power. And God will meet you the next day and every day; and never mind if in the practice of fellowship there comes failure sometimes. If you maintain your position and say: "Lord, I am going to expect Thee to do Thy utmost, and I am going to trust Thee day by day to keep me absolutely," your faith will grow stronger and stronger, and you will know the keeping power of God in unbrokenness.

And now the other side—*Believing*. "Kept by the power of God through faith." How must we look at this faith?

Let me say, first of all, that this *faith means utter impotence and helplessness before God*. At the bottom of all faith there is a feeling of helplessness. If I have a bit of business to transact, perhaps to buy a house, the conveyancer must do the work of getting the transfer of the property in my name, and making all the arrangements. I cannot do that work, and in trusting that agent I confess I cannot do it. And so faith always means helplessness. In many cases it means: I can do it with a great deal of trouble, but another can do it better. But in most cases it is utter helplessness; *another must do it for me*. And that is the secret of the spiritual life. A man must learn to say: "I give up everything; I have tried and longed, and thought and prayed, but failure has come. God has blessed me and helped me, but still, in the long run, there has been so much of sin and sadness." What a change comes when a man is thus broken down into utter helplessness and self-despair, and says: "I can do nothing!"

Remember Paul. He was living a blessed life, and he had been taken up into the third Heaven, and then the thorn in the flesh came, "a messenger of Satan to buffet me." And what happened? Paul could not understand it, and he prayed the Lord three times to take it away; but the Lord said, in effect: "No; it is possible that you might exalt yourself, and therefore I have sent you this trial to keep you weak and humble."

And Paul then learned a lesson that he never forgot, and that was—to rejoice in his infirmities. He said that the weaker he was the better it was for him, for when he was weak, he was strong in his Lord Christ.

Do you want to enter what people call "the higher life"? Then go a step lower down. I remember Dr. Boardman telling how that once he was invited by a gentleman to go to see some works where they made fine shot, and I believe the workmen did so by pouring down molten lead from a great height. This gentleman wanted to take Dr. Boardman up to the top of the tower to see how the work was done. The doctor came to the tower, he entered by the door, and began going upstairs; but when he had gone a few steps the gentleman called out: "That is the wrong way. You must come down this way; that stair is locked up."

The gentleman took him downstairs a good many steps, and there an elevator was ready to take him to the top; and he said: "I have learned a lesson that going down is often the best way to get up."

Ah, yes, God will have to bring us very low down; there will have to come upon us a sense of emptiness and despair and nothingness. It is when we sink down in utter helplessness that the everlasting God will reveal Himself in His power, and that our hearts will learn to trust God alone.

What is it that keeps us from trusting Him perfectly?

Many a one says: "I believe what you say, but there is one difficulty. If my trust were perfect and always abiding, all would come right, for I know God will honour trust. But how am I to get that trust?"

My answer is: "By the death of self. The great hindrance to trust is self-effort. So long as you have got your own wisdom and thoughts and strength, you cannot fully trust

God. But when God breaks you down, when everything begins to grow dim before your eyes, and you see that you understand nothing, then God is coming nigh, and if you will bow down in nothingness and wait upon God, He will become all."

As long as we are something, God cannot be all, and His omnipotence cannot do its full work. That is the beginning of faith—utter despair of self, a ceasing from man and everything on earth, and finding our hope in God alone.

And then, next, we must understand that *faith is rest*. In the beginning of the faith-life, faith is struggling; but as long as faith is struggling, faith has not attained its strength. But when faith in its struggling gets to the end of itself, and just throws itself upon God and rests on Him, then comes joy and victory.

Perhaps I can make it plainer if I tell the story of how the Keswick Convention began. Canon Battersby was an evangelical clergyman of the Church of England for more than twenty years, a man of deep and tender godliness, but he had not the consciousness of rest and victory over sin, and often was deeply sad at the thought of stumbling and failure and sin. When he heard about the possibility of victory, he felt it was desirable, but it was as if he could not attain it. On one occasion he heard an address on "Rest and Faith" from the story of the nobleman who came from Capernaum to Cana to ask Christ to heal his child. In the address it was shown that the nobleman believed that Christ could help him in a general way, but he came to Jesus a good deal by way of an experiment. He hoped Christ would help him, but he had not any assurance of that help. But what happened? When Christ said to him: "Go thy way, for thy child liveth," that man believed the word that Jesus spoke; he rested in that word. He had no proof that his child was well again, and he had to walk back seven hours' journey to Capernaum. He walked back, and on the way met his servant, and got the first news that the child was well, that at one o'clock on the afternoon of the previous day, at the very time that Jesus spoke to him, the fever left the child. That father rested upon the word of Jesus and His work, and he went down to Capernaum and found his child well; and he praised God, and became with his whole house a believer and disciple of Jesus.

Oh, friends, that is faith! When God comes to me with the promise of His keeping, and I have nothing on earth to trust in, I say to God: "Thy word is enough; kept by the power of God." That is faith, that is rest.

When Canon Battersby heard that address, he went home that night, and in the darkness of the night found rest. He rested on the word of Jesus. And the next morning, in the streets of Oxford, he said to a friend: "I have found it!" Then he went and told others, and asked that the Keswick Convention might be begun, and those at the convention with himself should testify simply what God had done.

It is a great thing when a man comes to rest on God's almighty power for every moment of his life, in prospect of temptations to temper and haste and anger and unlovingness and pride and sin. It is a great thing in prospect of these to enter into a covenant with the omnipotent Jehovah, not on account of anything that any man says, or of anything that my heart feels, but on the strength of the Word of God: "Kept by the power of God through faith."

Oh, let us say to God that we are going to prove Him to the very uttermost. Let us say: We ask Thee for nothing more than Thou canst give, but we want nothing less. Let us say: My God, let my life be a proof of what the omnipotent God can do. Let these be the two dispositions of our souls every day—deep helplessness, and simple, childlike rest.

That brings me to just one more thought in regard to faith—*faith implies fellowship with God.*

Many people want to take the Word and believe that, and they find they cannot believe it. Ah, no! you cannot separate God from His Word. No goodness or power can be received separate from God, and if you want to get into this life of godliness, you *must* take time for fellowship with God.

People sometimes tell me: "My life is one of such scurry and bustle that I have no time for fellowship with God." A dear missionary said to me: "People do not know how we missionaries are tempted. I get up at five o'clock in the morning, and there are the natives waiting for their orders for work. Then I have to go to the school and spend hours there; and then there is other work, and sixteen hours rush along, and I hardly get time to be alone with God."

Ah! there is the want. I pray you, remember two things. I have not told you to trust the omnipotence of God as a thing, and I have not told you to trust the Word of God as a written book, but I have told you to go to the God of omnipotence and the God of the Word. Deal with God as that nobleman dealt with the living Christ. Why was he able to believe the word that Christ spoke to him?

Because in the very eyes and tones and voice of Jesus, the Son of God, he saw and heard something which made him feel that he could trust Him. And that is what Christ can do for you and me. Do not try to stir and arouse faith from within. How often I have tried to do that, and made a fool of myself! You cannot stir up faith from the depths of your heart. Leave your heart, and look into the face of Christ, and listen to what He tells you about how He will keep you. Look up into the face of your loving Father, and take time every day with Him, and begin a new life with the deep emptiness and poverty of a man who has got nothing, and who wants to get everything from Him— with the deep restfulness of a man who rests on the living God, the omnipotent Jehovah—and try God, and prove Him if He will not open the windows of Heaven and pour out a blessing that there shall not be room to receive it.

I close by asking if you are willing to experience to the very full the heavenly keeping for the heavenly inheritance? Robert Murray M'Cheyne says, somewhere: "Oh, God, make me as holy as a pardoned sinner can be made." And if that prayer is in your heart, come now, and let us enter into a covenant with the everlasting and omnipotent Jehovah afresh, and in great helplessness, but in great restfulness place ourselves in His hands. And then as we enter into our covenant, let us have the one prayer—that we may believe fully that the everlasting God is going to be our Companion, holding our hand every moment of the day; our Keeper, watching over us without a moment's interval; our Father, delighting to reveal Himself in our souls always. He has the power to let the sunshine of His love be with us all the day. Do not be afraid because you have got your business that you cannot have God with you always. Learn the lesson that the natural sun shines upon you all the day, and you enjoy its light, and wherever you are you have got the sun; God takes care that it shines upon you. And God will take care that His own divine light shines upon you, and that you shall abide in that light, if you will only trust Him for it. Let us trust God to do that with a great and entire trust.

Ere we join in prayer, listen to my last words. Here is the omnipotence of God, and here is faith reaching out to the measure of that omnipotence. Shall we not say: "All that that omnipotence can do, I am going to trust my God for"? Are not the two sides of this heavenly life wonderful? God's omnipotence covers me, and my will in its littleness rests in that omnipotence, and rejoices in it!

> Moment by moment, I'm kept in His love;
> Moment by moment, I've life from above;
> Looking to Jesus, the glory doth shine;
> Moment by moment, Oh, Lord, I am Thine!

14

"Ye Are the Branches"

I have been asked to speak to Christian workers, and the one thought that is in my heart in looking on the faces of all these beloved Christian workers is this—that everything depends on our being right ourselves in Christ. If I want good apples, I must have a good apple tree; and if I care for the health of the apple tree, the apple tree will give me good apples. And it is just so with our Christian life and work. *If our life with Christ be right*, all will come right. There may be the need of instruction and suggestion and help and training in the different departments of the work; all that has value. But in the long run, the greatest essential is to have the full life in Christ—in other words, to have Christ in us, working through us. I know how much there often is to disturb us, or to cause anxious questionings; but the Master has such a blessing for every one of us, and such perfect peace and rest, and such joy and strength, if we can only come into, and be kept in, the right attitude toward Him.

I will take my text from the parable of the Vine and the Branches, in John 15:5: *"I am the vine, ye are the branches."* Especially these words: *"Ye are the branches."*

What a simple thing it is to be a branch, the branch of a

tree, or the branch of a vine! The branch grows out of the vine, or out of the tree, and there it lives and grows, and in due time, bears fruit. It has no responsibility except just to receive from the root and stem sap and nourishment. And if we only by the Holy Spirit knew our relationship to Jesus Christ, our work would be changed into the brightest and most heavenly thing upon earth. Instead of there ever being soul-weariness or exhaustion, our work would be like a new experience, linking us to Jesus as nothing else can. For, alas! is it not often true that our work comes between us and Jesus? What folly! The very work that He has to do in me, and I for Him, I take up in such a way that it separates me from Christ. Many a labourer in the vineyard has complained that he has too much work, and not time for close communion with Jesus, and that his usual work weakens his inclination for prayer, and that his too much intercourse with men darkens the spiritual life. Sad thought, that the bearing of fruit should separate the branch from the vine! That must be because we have looked upon our work as something other than the branch bearing fruit. May God deliver us from every false thought about the Christian life.

Now, just a few thoughts about **this blessed branch-life.**

In the first place, it is a *life of absolute dependence.* The branch has nothing; it just depends upon the vine for everything. That word *absolute dependence* is one of the most solemn and precious of thoughts. A great German theologian wrote two large volumes some years ago to show that the whole of Calvin's theology is summed up in that one principle of *absolute dependence upon God*; and he was right. Another great writer has said that *absolute, unalterable dependence upon God alone* is the essence of the religion of angels, and should be that of men also. God is everything to the angels, and He is willing to be everything to the Christian. If I can learn every moment of the day to depend upon God, everything will come right. You will get the higher life if you depend absolutely upon God.

Now, here we find it with the vine and the branches. Every vine you ever see, or every bunch of grapes that comes upon your table, let it remind you that the branch is absolutely dependent on the vine. The vine has to do the work, and the branch enjoys the fruit of it.

What has the vine to do? It has to do a great work. It has to send its roots out into the soil and hunt under the ground—the roots often extend a long way out—for nourishment, and to drink in the moisture. Put certain elements of manure in certain directions, and the vine sends its roots there, and then in its roots or stems it turns the moisture and manure into that special sap which is to make the fruit that is borne. The vine does the work, and the branch has just to receive from the vine the sap, which is changed into grapes. I have been told that at Hampton Court, London, there is a vine that sometimes bore a couple of thousand bunches of grapes, and people were astonished at its large growth and rich fruitage. Afterward it was discovered what was the cause of it. Not so very far away runs the River Thames, and the vine had stretched its roots away hundreds of yards under the ground, until it had come to the riverside, and there in all the rich slime of the riverbed it had found rich nourishment, and obtained moisture, and the roots had drown the sap all that distance up and up into the vine, and as a result there was the abundant, rich harvest. The vine had the work to do, and the branches had just to depend upon the vine, and receive what it gave.

Is that literally true of my Lord Jesus? Must I understand that when I have to work, when I have to preach a sermon, or address a Bible class, or to go out and visit the poor, neglected ones, that all the responsibility of the work is on Christ?

That is exactly what Christ wants you to understand. Christ wants that in all your work, the very foundation should be the simple, blessed consciousness: Christ must care for all.

And *how does He fulfil the trust of that dependence?* He does it by sending down the Holy Spirit—not now and then only as a special gift, for remember the relationship between the vine and the branches is such that hourly, daily, unceasingly there is the living connection maintained. The sap does not flow for a time, and then stop, and then flow again, but from moment to moment the sap flows from the vine to the branches. And just so, my Lord Jesus wants me to take that blessed position as a worker, and morning by morning and day by day and hour by hour and step by step, in every work I have to go out to just to abide before Him in the simple utter helplessness of one who knows nothing, and is nothing, and can do nothing. Oh, beloved workers, study that word *nothing*. You sometimes sing: "Oh, to be nothing, nothing"; but have you really studied that word and prayed every day, and worshiped God, in the light of it? Do you know the blessedness of that word nothing?

If I am something, then God is not everything; but when I become *nothing*, God can become *all*, and the everlasting God in Christ can reveal Himself fully. That is the higher life. We need to become nothing. Someone has well said that the seraphim and cherubim are flames of fire because they know they are nothing, and they allow God to put His fullness and His glory and brightness into them. Oh, become nothing in deep reality, and, as a worker, study only one thing—to become poorer and lower and more helpless, that Christ may work all in you.

Workers, here is your first lesson: learn to be nothing, learn to be helpless. The man who has got something is not absolutely dependent; but the man who has got nothing is absolutely dependent. Absolute dependence upon God is the secret of all power in work. The branch has nothing but what it gets from the vine, and you and I can have nothing but what we get from Jesus.

But secondly, the life of the branch is not only a life of entire dependence, but *of deep restfulness*. That little branch, if it could think, and if it could feel, and if it could speak—that branch away in Hampton Court vine, or on some of the million vines that we have in South Africa, in our sunny land—if we could have a little branch here today to talk to us, and if we could say: "Come, branch of the vine, I want to learn from you how I can be a true branch of the living Vine," what would it answer? The little branch would whisper: "Man, I hear that you are wise, and I know that you can do a great many wonderful things. I know you have much strength and wisdom given to you but I have one lesson for you. With all your hurry and effort in Christ's work you never prosper. The first thing you need is to come and rest in your Lord Jesus. That is what I do. Since I grew out of that vine I have spent years and years, and all I have done is just to rest in the vine. When the time of spring came I had no anxious thought or care. The vine began to pour its sap into me, and to give the bud and leaf. And when the time of summer came I had no care, and in the great heat I trusted the vine to bring moisture to keep me fresh. And in the time of harvest, when the owner came to pluck the grapes, I had no care. If there was anything in the grapes not good, the owner never blamed the branch, the blame was always on the vine. And if you would be a true branch of Christ, the living Vine, just rest on Him. Let Christ bear the responsibility."

You say: "Won't that make me slothful?" I tell you it will not. No one who learns to rest upon the living Christ can become slothful, for the closer your contact with Christ the more of the Spirit of His zeal and love will be borne in upon you. But, oh, begin to work in the midst of your entire dependence by adding to that *deep restfulness*. A man sometimes tries and tries to be dependent upon Christ, but he worries himself about this absolute dependence; he tries and he cannot get it. But let him sink down into entire restfulness every day.

> In Thy strong hand I lay me down.
> So shall the work be done;
> For who can work so wondrously
> As the Almighty One?

Worker, take your place every day at the feet of Jesus, in the blessed peace and rest that come from the knowledge—

> I have no care, my cares are His!
> I have no fear, He cares for all my fears.

Come, children of God, and understand that it is the Lord Jesus who wants to work through you. You complain of the want of fervent love. It will come from Jesus. He will give the divine love in your heart with which you can love people. That is the meaning of the assurance: "The love of God is shed abroad in our hearts by the Holy Spirit"; and of that other word: "The love of Christ constraineth us." Christ can give you a fountain of love, so that you cannot help loving the most wretched and the most ungrateful, or those who have wearied you hitherto. Rest in Christ, who can give wisdom and strength, and you do not know how that restfulness will often prove to be the very best part of your message. You plead with people and you argue, and they get the idea: "There is a man arguing and striving with me." They only feel: "Here are two men dealing with each other." But if you will let the deep rest of God come over you, the rest in Christ Jesus, the peace and rest and holiness of Heaven, that restfulness will bring a blessing to the heart, even more than the words you speak.

But a third thought. *The branch teaches a lesson of much fruitfulness*. The Lord Jesus Christ repeated that word *fruit* often in that parable. He spoke, first, of *fruit*, and then of *more fruit*, and then of much fruit. Yes, you are ordained not only to bear fruit, but to bear *much fruit*.

"Herein is my Father glorified, *that ye bear much fruit.*"
In the first place, Christ said: "I am the Vine, and my
Father is the Husbandman. My Father is the Husbandman
who has charge of me and you." He who will watch over
the connection between Christ and the branches is God;
and it is in the power of God through Christ we are to bear
fruit.

O Christians, you know this world is perishing for the
want of workers. And it wants not only more workers—the
workers are saying, some more earnestly than others: "We
need not only more workers, but we need our workers
to have a new power, a different life; that we workers
should be able to bring more blessing." Children of God,
I appeal to you. You know what trouble you take, say, in
a case of sickness. You have a beloved friend apparently
in danger of death, and nothing can refresh that friend so
much as a few grapes, and they are out of season; but
what trouble you will take to get the grapes that are to be
the nourishment of this dying friend! And, oh, there are
around you people who never go to church, and so many
who go to church, but do not know Christ. And yet the
heavenly grapes, the grapes of Eshcol, the grapes of the
heavenly Vine are not to be had at any price, except as the
child of God bears them out of his inner life in fellowship
with Christ. Except the children of God are filled with the
sap of the heavenly Vine, except they are filled with the
Holy Spirit and the love of Jesus, they cannot bear much
of the real heavenly grape. We all confess there is a great
deal of work, a great deal of preaching and teaching and
visiting, a great deal of machinery, a great deal of earnest
effort of every kind; but there is not much manifestation

of the power of God in it.

What is wanting? There is wanting the close connection between the worker and the heavenly Vine. Christ, the heavenly Vine, has blessings that He could pour on tens of thousands who are perishing. Christ, the heavenly Vine, has power to provide the heavenly grapes. But "Ye are the branches," and you cannot bear heavenly fruit unless you are in close connection with Jesus Christ.

Do not confound work and fruit. There may be a good deal of work for Christ that is not the fruit of the heavenly Vine. Do not seek for work only. Oh! study this question of fruit-bearing. It means the very life and the very power and the very spirit and the very love within the heart of the Son of God—it means the heavenly Vine Himself coming into your heart and mine.

You know there are different sorts of grapes, each with a different name, and every vine provides exactly that peculiar aroma and juice which gives the grape its particular flavour and taste. Just so, there is in the heart of Christ Jesus a life, and a love, and a Spirit, and a blessing, and a power for men, that are entirely heavenly and divine, and that will come down into our hearts. Stand in close connection with the heavenly Vine and say: "Lord Jesus, nothing less than the sap that flows through Thyself, nothing less than the Spirit of Thy divine life is what we ask. Lord Jesus, I pray Thee let Thy Spirit flow through me in all my work for Thee."

I tell you again that the sap of the heavenly Vine is nothing but the Holy Spirit. The Holy Spirit is the life of the heavenly Vine, and what you must get from Christ is nothing less than a strong inflow of the Holy Spirit.

You need it exceedingly, and you want nothing more than that. Remember that. Do not expect Christ to give a bit of strength here, and a bit of blessing yonder, and a bit of help over there. As the vine does its work in giving its own peculiar sap to the branch, so expect Christ to give His own Holy Spirit into your heart, and then you will bear much fruit. And if you have only begun to bear fruit, and are listening to the word of Christ in the parable, "more fruit," "much fruit," remember that in order that you should bear more fruit you just require more of Jesus in your life and heart.

We ministers of the Gospel, how we are in danger of getting into a condition of *work, work, work!* And we pray over it, but the freshness and buoyancy and joy of the heavenly life are not always present. Let us seek to understand that the life of the branch is a life of much fruit, because it is a life rooted in Christ, the living, heavenly Vine.

A fourth thought. *The life of the branch is a life of close communion.* Let us again ask: What has the branch to do? You know that precious, inexhaustible word that Christ used: *Abide.* Your life is to be an abiding life. And how is the abiding to be? It is to be just like the branch in the vine, abiding every minute of the day. There are the branches, in close communion, in unbroken communion, with the vine, from January to December. And cannot I live every day—it is to me an almost terrible thing that we should ask the question—cannot I live in abiding communion with the heavenly Vine?

You say: "But I am so much occupied with other things."

You may have ten hours' hard work daily, during which your brain has to be occupied with temporal things; God orders it so. But the abiding work is the work of the *heart*, not of the brain, the work of the heart clinging to and resting in Jesus, a work in which the Holy Spirit links us to Christ Jesus. Oh, do believe that deeper down than the brain, deep down in the inner life, you can abide in Christ, so that every moment you are free the consciousness will come: "Blessed Jesus, I am still in Thee."

If you will learn for a time to put aside other work and to get into this abiding contract with the heavenly Vine, you will find that fruit will come.

What is the application to our life of this abiding communion? What does it mean?

It means close fellowship with Christ in secret prayer. I am sure there are Christians who do long for the higher life, and who sometimes have got a great blessing, and have at times found a great inflow of heavenly joy and a great outflow of heavenly gladness; and yet after a time it has passed away. They have not understood that close personal actual communion with Christ is an absolute necessity for daily life. Take time to be alone with Christ. Nothing in Heaven or earth can free you from the necessity for that, if you are to be happy and holy Christians.

Oh! how many Christians look upon it as a burden and a tax, and a duty, and a difficulty to be often alone with God! That is the great hindrance to our Christian life everywhere. We need more quiet fellowship with God, and I tell you in the name of the heavenly Vine that you cannot be healthy branches, branches into which the heavenly sap can flow, unless you take plenty of time for communion with God. If you are not willing to sacrifice time to get alone with Him, and to give Him time every day to work in you, and to keep up the link of connection between you and Himself, He cannot give you that blessing of His unbroken fellowship. Jesus Christ asks you to live in close communion with Him. Let every heart say: "O Christ, it is this I long for, it is this I choose." And He will gladly give it to you.

And then my last thought. *The life of the branch is a life of absolute surrender.* This word, absolute surrender, is a great and solemn word, and I believe we do not understand its meaning. But yet the little branch preaches it. "Have you anything to do, little branch, besides bearing grapes?"

"No, *nothing.*"

"Are you fit for nothing?"

"Fit for nothing!" The Bible says that a bit of vine cannot even be used as a pen; it is fit for nothing but to be burned.

"And now, what do you understand, little branch, about your relationship to the vine?"

"My relationship is just this: I am utterly given up to the vine, and the vine can give me as much or as little sap as it chooses. Here I am at its disposal and the vine can do with me what it likes."

Oh, friends, we need this absolute surrender to the Lord Jesus Christ. The more I speak, the more I feel that this is one of the most difficult points to make clear, and one of the most important and needful points to explain—what this absolute surrender is. It is often an easy thing for a man or a number of men to come out and offer themselves up to God for entire consecration, and to say: "Lord, it is my desire to give up myself entirely to Thee." That is of great value, and often brings very rich blessing. But the one question I ought to study quietly is, What is *meant* by absolute surrender?

It means that, as literally as Christ was given up entirely to God, I am given up entirely to Christ. Is that too strong? Some think so. Some think that never can be; that just as entirely and absolutely as Christ gave up His life to do nothing but seek the Father's pleasure, and depend on the Father absolutely and entirely, I am to do nothing but to seek the pleasure of Christ. But that is actually true. Christ Jesus came to breathe His own Spirit into us, to make us find our very highest happiness in living entirely for God, just as He did. Oh, beloved brethren, if that is the case, then I ought to say: "Yes, as true as it is of that little branch of the vine, so true, by God's grace, I would have it to be of me. I would live day by day that Christ may be able to do with me what He will."

Ah! here comes the terrible mistake that lies at the bottom of so much of our own religion. A man thinks: "I have my business and family duties, and my relationships as a citizen, and all this I cannot change. And now alongside all this I am to take in religion and the service of God, as something that will keep me from sin. God help me to perform my duties properly!"

This is not right. When Christ came, He came and bought the sinner with His blood. If there was a slave market here and I were to buy a slave, I should take that slave away to my own house from his old surroundings, and he would live at my house as my personal property, and I could order him about all the day. And if he were a faithful slave, he would live as having no will and no interests of his own, his one care being to promote the well-being and honour of his master. And in like manner I, who have been bought with the blood of Christ, have been bought to live every day with one thought—How can I please my Master?

Oh, we find the Christian life so difficult because we seek for God's blessing while we live in our own will. We should be glad to live the Christian life according to our own liking. We make our own plans and choose our own work, and then we ask the Lord Jesus to come in and take care that sin shall not conquer us too much, and that we shall not go too far wrong; we ask Him to come in and give us so much of His blessing. But our relationship to Jesus ought to be such that we are entirely at His disposal, and every day come to Him humbly and straightforwardly and say: "Lord, is there anything in me that is not according to Thy will, that has not been ordered by Thee, or that is not entirely given up to Thee?"

Oh, if we would wait and wait patiently, I tell you what the result would be. There would spring up a relationship between us and Christ so close and so tender that we should afterward be amazed at how we formerly could have lived with the idea: "I am surrendered to Christ." We should feel how far distant our intercourse with Him had previously been, and that He can, and does indeed, come and take actual possession of us, and gives unbroken fellowship all the day. The branch calls us to absolute surrender.

I do not speak this afternoon so much about the giving

up of sins. There are people who need that, people who have got violent tempers, bad habits, and actual sins which they from time to time commit, and which they have never given up into the very bosom of the Lamb of God. I pray you, if you are branches of the living Vine, do not keep one sin back. I know there are a great many difficulties about this question of holiness. I know that all do not think exactly the same with regard to it. That would be to me a matter of comparative indifference if I could see that all are honestly longing to be free from every sin. But I am afraid that unconsciously there are in hearts often compromises with the idea that we cannot be without sin, we must sin a little every day; we cannot help it. Oh, that people would actually cry to God: "Lord, do keep me from sin!" Give yourself utterly to Jesus, and ask Him to do His very utmost for you in keeping you from sin.

There is a great deal in our work, in our church and our surroundings that we found in the world when we were born into it, and it has grown all around us, and we think that it is all right, it cannot be changed. We do not come to the Lord Jesus and ask Him about it. Oh! I advise you, Christians, *bring everything into relationship with Jesus* and say: "Lord, everything in my life has to be in most complete harmony with my position as a branch of Thee, the blessed Vine."

Let your surrender to Christ be absolute. I do not understand that word *surrender* fully; it gets new meanings every now and then; it enlarges immensely from time to time. But I advise you to speak it out: "Absolute surrender to Thee, O Christ, is what I have chosen." And Christ will show you what is not according to His mind, and lead you on to deeper and higher blessedness.

In conclusion, let me gather up all in one sentence. Christ Jesus said: "I am the Vine, ye are the branches." In other words: "I, the living One who have so completely given myself to you, am the Vine. You cannot trust me too much. I am the Almighty Worker, full of a divine life and power." You are the branches of the Lord Jesus Christ. If there is in your heart the consciousness that you are not a strong, healthy, fruit-bearing branch, not closely linked with Jesus, not living in Him as you should be—then listen to Him say: "I am the Vine, I will receive you, I will draw you to myself, I will bless you, I will strengthen you, I will fill you with my Spirit. I, the Vine, have taken you to be my branches, I have given myself utterly to you; children, give yourselves utterly to me. I have surrendered myself as God absolutely to you; I became man and died for you that I might be entirely yours. Come and surrender yourselves entirely to be mine."

What shall our answer be? Oh, let it be a prayer from the depths of our heart, that the living Christ may take each one of us and link us close to Himself. Let our prayer be that He, the living Vine, shall so link each of us to Himself that we shall go away with our hearts singing: "He is my Vine, and I am His branch—I want nothing more—now I have the everlasting Vine." Then, when you get alone with Him, worship and adore Him, praise and trust Him, love Him and wait for His love. "Thou art my Vine, and I am Thy branch. It is enough, my soul is satisfied."

Glory to His blessed name!

RHP Essential Classics

T. AUSTIN-SPARKS
The School of Christ
The inner working of the Holy Spirit

E. M. BOUNDS
Power Through Prayer
A stirring exhortation to pray

JOHN BUNYAN
The Pilgrim's Progress
The classic allegory of the Christian life

CHARLES FINNEY
Revival
God's way of revival

A. P. FITT
D. L. Moody
The life of the great evangelist

ROY HESSION
The Calvary Road
The way of personal revival
Our Nearest Kinsman
The message of hope from the book of Ruth
Not I, but Christ
The Christian's relationship with Jesus explained from the life of David
The Power of God's Grace
The way of peace, joy and genuine revival
We Would See Jesus
Seeing in Jesus everything we need
When I Saw Him
Renewing your vision of Jesus
My Calvary Road
Roy Hession tells his own story

Please ask for these titles at your local Christian bookshop

RHP Essential Classics

F. & M. HOWARD TAYLOR
The Biography of James Hudson Taylor
The life of a man of God

DAVID WILKERSON
Hallowed Be Thy Names
Knowing God through His names
Hungry For More of Jesus
The way of intimacy with Christ

ANDREW MURRAY
Absolute Surrender
A call to radical, Spirit-filled Christianity
The Full Blessing of Pentecost
Power from on High
Humility
The way to victory in the Christian life
The True Vine
Fruitfulness and stability in Jesus
Waiting on God
Allowing the power of God into our lives and ministries

OSWALD J. SMITH
The Enduement of Power
Being filled with the Holy Spirit
The Man God Uses
How anyone can be used powerfully by God
The Revival We Need
A heart-stirring cry for revival

R. A. TORREY
How to Pray
Praying with power and authority
How to Study the Bible
Profit and pleasure from the Word of God

Please ask for these titles at your local Christian bookshop